# Enrichment

## *A History of the Public Library in the United States in the Twentieth Century*

Lowell A. Martin

The Scarecrow Press, Inc.
Lanham, Maryland & Oxford
1998

SCARECROW PRESS, INC.

Published in the United States of America
by Scarecrow Press, Inc.
4720 Boston Way
Lanham, Maryland 20706

4 Pleydell Gardens
Kent CT20 2DN, England



British Library Cataloguing in Publication Information Available

**Library of Congress Cataloging-in-Publication Data**

Martin, Lowell Arthur, 1912–
Enrichment : a history of the public library in the United States in the twentieth century / Lowell A. Martin.
p. cm.
Includes bibliographical references and index.
ISBN 0-8108-3403-0 (cloth : alk. paper)
1. Public libraries—United States—History—20th century.
I. Title.
Z731.M326 1998
027.473'09'04—dc21 97-43171

∞ ™ The paper used in this publication meets the minimum requirements of American National Standard for Information Sciences—Permanence of Paper for Printed Library Materials, ANSI Z39.48–1984. Manufactured in the United States of America.

*To My Wife,*
*Partner and Companion*
*for over Sixty Years*

# Contents

# Introduction

We tend to think of history in terms of very visible and notable events—a war, a revolution, a new leader, a catastrophe. But the most important and durable currents may run below the surface, in the birth and growth of new goals, new values, new attitudes. When these deeper changes are shared by wide segments of the populace, the result is genuine historical change.

Two profound currents have characterized the nineteenth and twentieth centuries in America: democracy and capitalism. Both of these favor the public library.

Democracy provides a rationale for the institution. Democracy needs an agency of continuing education, a source of facts and background for informed citizenship. It also needs a means for individual development, so citizens can reach their full potential. And it needs a source of personal enrichment in a growing technological age. This volume will examine the extent to which the public library has achieved these purposes.

Capitalism requires trained workers and responsive customers. On the other hand, the libraries need capitalism to produce wealth and government revenue in order to build buildings and acquire and organize collections. This volume will describe the relationship between economic growth and the public library and the limitations on library response in times of recession and depression.

These two institutions—democracy and capitalism—are sometimes opposing forces. The first frees people, protects liberty, gives all an opportunity, and warms the heart. The second provides power to some and denies it to others. The two ideas meet and react, creating a continuing tension, making for equality and inequality. It is almost surprising that they have existed together, in the same society, through the past two hundred years. The public library serves both and gains from both. This is why it has survived and prospered.

The public library appeared in the nineteenth century from this background (as we will shortly see from a brief summary) and grew and diversified in the twentieth century in response to a maturing country. The last one hundred years are the subject of this volume.

The effort here will be to show the public library as a natural outgrowth of America in the making. This is social history and institutional history. Hopefully it will show the development of the institution in some detail and also its relation to the positive elements in its environment. Given the country, the public library had to become what it is.

There are three questions which readers have in mind in approaching a new book—why this volume?, why this author?, and why this organization of the material?

The story of the origins of the public library in the nineteenth century has been well documented (see for example Jesse Shera's *Foundations of the Public Library*). The great expansion of the institution in the twentieth century, on the other hand, has not been pulled together in a single treatment. Many fragments of recent history exist in journal articles, in academic dissertations, and in the records of individual libraries. The aim in this volume is to provide an overall account, a synthesis, for an agency that has made a place in American life and contributed to the growth of the country.

This is an effort not only to set down notable events in public-library development during these crowning years, but also to probe for underlying trends that either furthered or deterred the growth of the institution. This is social-cultural history in the tradition of Lawrence Cremin's *Transformation of the School* and Philip Altback's *Higher Education in American Society*. The library in society, cause, and effect—that is the purpose.

The aim is not solely to praise the growth and success of the institution, but also to note problems and uncertainties where they appeared along the way, to show the public library when it hit and when it missed the mark.

As for this author, I have lived through much of the century. I was born in 1912, held my first library job in 1927, and completed my last commissioned study of a library in 1985. I have observed and been involved with the institution for eight decades, from the first spurt of growth in the 1920s to its uncertain prospect at the end of the century. I have been book shelver, library clerk, branch librarian, administrative assistant, professor and dean in library schools, and consultant to a dozen city and state library systems.

In the citation for honorary membership granted by the American Library Association in 1979 I am described as "a major contributor to the library movement of the century." Whether this is justified praise or hyperbole is for others to say. Now I am on the sidelines, providing a little perspective.

An individual's appraisal of an institution is influenced by his or her personal values, by deep-set aspirations and inhibitions. Much of my personal identity has derived from the public library. Is this why I am such a mixture of optimism and criticism?

So here is one participant's view of the growth of the agency. Another observer might be more disposed to sing its glories—or to probe its shortcomings. It is hoped that this interpretation has balance, a sense of the marvelous achievements on the one hand, combined with a recognition of missed opportunities and of diffuse and overambitious purposes on the other hand.

The account here is organized chronologically with the century divided into six segments, from the first era up to World War I through to the current two decades leading to the turn of the next century. Within each segment there is a brief background summary of the main social, cultural, and political characteristics of the time. Then the broad thrust of library service in each period is briefly reviewed, followed by more detailed examination of notable professional developments in the same years. Some concerns will recur in different periods—the purposes of the institution, for example, will come to the fore at various times—as will certain services as they grew and declined—youth service and adult education, for example. Before the six segments in the twentieth century there will be a summary of the legacy from the nineteenth century, for the modern library grew out of its legacy and its precursors. The public library is an agency with three characteristics: maintained by the government, supported by tax money, and open free to all. It will take many forms, from the bookmobile in a remote rural area to a research center in a city, from a children's collection in the slums to a cultural center in a comfortable suburb. There may be one staff member or a thousand, books alone or various electronic communication channels. In the end the agency may be more computer terminals than print, but the essentials will remain: government auspices, public money, and open access.

This book is not a paean to the success of the public library nor solely a critique of its shortcomings. Inevitably, along the way, the triumphs will emerge and also the lost opportunities. But the object here is to tell the story of the institution—straight and balanced—and perhaps from this account the reader can predict its role in the next century.

# 1

# The Legacy of the Nineteenth Century

It is fascinating to note the various efforts of the public library to be born in the eighteenth century and on through the nineteenth, from the ill-fated project of Thomas Bray, an Anglican cleric in the early 1700s, through such permutations as the "Book Boat" on the Erie Canal and the railroad reading rooms in Ohio from 1865 to 1900. The early public library movement was a vigorous youngster who would grow to a productive adulthood.

In the decades before 1900, the public library movement was energized by pronouncements from leaders who sought to carry the people along. Horace Mann asked a pointed question; "after the rising generation have acquired habits of intelligent reading in our schools, what shall they read? For with no books to read, the power of reading will be useless."[1] Henry Barnard answered by proposing that

> A library of good books should be provided in every village to help the old and the young better to understand the history and condition of the world and the country in which they live, their own nature, and their relations and duties to society themselves, and their Creator.[2]

Most of the early predecessors of the public library can be summarized under four headings: parish libraries, school district libraries, social libraries, and circulating libraries. Then some anomalies must be added around the edges, such as the collections assembled by mill girls working in New England factories and the Sunday school libraries.

Parish libraries in America and England originally were the idea of Reverend Thomas Bray back in the eighteenth century. The church, as he saw it, would acquire books and make them available not just to clergy and parishioners but also to the general public. Emphasis was on religious material but extended to literature and the classics, because he had an educational goal. Bray also encouraged circulation of volumes, so readers could study them at home. Seventy such collections were established in America.[3] He hoped to get public financing, but this seldom occurred. Parish libraries declined after Bray's death in 1730. Several ingredients of the public library can be seen in this early effort: variety in holdings, general access to the public, home circulation, and a desire for public financing.

School district libraries open to the general public were the dream of Horace Mann. He got the idea enacted into New York State law in 1835. Now we had another essential of the public library, tax support. But the concept did not flourish. This was before the consolidation movement for school districts, and there were no less than eleven thousand such districts in New York State at the time, many with one-room schools; the governmental and financial base was too small. In addition, the libraries were imposed from above by state law and did not rise from the desire or effort of potential readers.[4] They were neither fish nor fowl, not school libraries nor public libraries.

This was not the case with social libraries, which were started by and supported by those who used them. The concept goes back to Benjamin Franklin and his Junto, a debating society. He said in 1730 that by "clubbing books to a Common Library, we should each of us have the advantage of using the books of all the other members, which would be nearly as beneficial as if we owned the whole."[5] By 1742 this grew into the idea of a "subscription" library for a wider group of readers, in which each participant would make an up-front investment to buy stock and then provide annual subscriptions to maintain additions to the collections.

The idea took a variety of subforms. There were mercantile libraries for young businessmen and mechanic libraries for young technicians who took the initiative and paid the costs. Collections were not limited to business or technical books but extended to material for general education.[6] The Mercantile Library of San Francisco, as one example, added 2,000 books in 1876 and had a circulation of 80,000. The Young Men's Mercantile Library Association of Cincinnati continued into the 1950s, and had 800 members with a collection of 20,000 volumes at that time.

The pattern appealed to other groups, not necessarily of the masculine gender. Women's groups were often the instigators; they started fifty-nine of the ninety-three social libraries established in California between 1878 and 1910.[7] In time there were over one thousand such agencies in the country. In fact memberships in such a group became a sign of social standing, and some of the subscription libraries continued well after regular public libraries became common.

"Circulating" libraries were the commercial ventures of booksellers and printers. Call them rental agencies, for they provided a collection from which individuals could borrow by paying so much a day or week. Literally several thousand such collections sprouted in the nineteenth century, catering to a literate population that was reaching for something to read. An intriguing variation was the Book Boat that moved along the Erie Canal after it opened in the 1820s; people came to the dock and rented books for a day or two, read them rapidly, and returned them before the vessel took off for its next stop.

The content of collections in the social (self-organized) libraries on the one hand and circulating (rental) libraries on the other differed sharply. The first had more substantial literature, for the motivation behind them was educational in the broad sense, with people seeking to understand history, religion or current affairs. The commercial provisions, in contrast, stressed the growing interest in romance and recreational reading. We will see both strains in the public libraries as they appeared.

Other more limited sprouting of libraries open to the public occurred in Sunday-school collections and the railroad reading rooms previously mentioned. This last variation had a worthwhile purpose—to give people waiting for trains something useful to do—but it caught on and readers simply took the books on the train as they continued their journey, thus depleting the collections. Nor should one omit the collections accumulated by the mill girls of New England, young women who came off the farms to work in the textile mills.[8] Everyone wanted to get into the act. Altogether it had been a remarkable flowering, a people's movement.

For all the local enthusiasm which engendered the social libraries, one by one they declined and vanished. They lost their moving spirits or their financial support in periods of economic decline. And growing up next to them was the form that would come to predominate, the public library.

Clearly the multiple patterns that nineteenth century efforts took demonstrate that the emergence of the public library was a grass-roots movement. This was not an idea of a small group of ideologues or a notion of some government officials. It was an institution sought by various groups in the population, and as a consequence, in time it was accepted by public officials as a legitimate use of tax money. No doubt, at a deeper level, it was influenced by the needs of an expanding country, by a community dedicated to democracy, and by a belief in education for all as a means of prosperity and advancement.

The appearance of so many social libraries, and their organization by local women's groups and by young businessmen and technicians, support the conclusion that this was a democratic movement aimed at self-improvement. But, when we trace the arrival of the public library as we know it today, we will come on a revisionist interpretation of the genesis of the institution. This view holds that the agency, at least in the beginning, was fostered by the "gentry" to help keep control of rebellious workers caught in the industrial constraints of the later years of the nineteenth century. This interpretation will be examined in reviewing the mission of the public library in the 1900–17 period.

Jesse Shera, in his notable *Foundations of the Public Library*[9], cites a variety of influences that combined to produce the public library. The underlying economic strength of the country had advanced to the point where surplus money could be found for this public enterprise. Public education was coming into place, producing a literate population. There was an upswelling movement for self-education, as evidenced in the widespread appearance of lyceum groups and literary societies. And, as economic opportunity opened up, young men sought information about and training for emerging careers.

To this day, where government officers at any level face the need for retrenchment and cutting of services, they hesitate when it comes to the public library, for the agency is seen as an instrument of that individual self-development in which conservatives as well as liberals believe. Indeed, a question which will arise as we proceed with this history is whether the institution is seen by both the population at large and by officialdom as achieving more social goals than it actually accomplishes. The public library is seen as a venerable institution even though it may be treated financially as a neglected institution. And because the concept was so widely accepted, we will see small public libraries started in every hamlet and isolated gathering of people, so that the agency later had to go through a period of reorganization to seek an adequate financial and territorial base for service.

Thus it can rightly be said that the foundation of twentieth century library service had been laid by 1900. The several kinds of libraries had emerged and been defined. Among them was an institution of the people, the public library as we know it today, an agency of government, open to all, and financed by tax money. More than a foundation, there was a kind of blueprint for the structure to be built, which would in part be followed in the next hundred years. Most cities had taken the step by the turn of the century.[10]

A person familiar with public libraries in 1900 would recognize the essentials in the contemporary agency at the end of the twentieth century. At the same time, such an individual would probably be amazed at the size it had achieved, would be astonished at technological changes that had been adopted, and would still wonder at the multiplicity of purposes that it was trying to serve.

Only parts of the blueprint had been implemented by 1900. The structure would have to grow much bigger, trained professionals would have to be found to operate it, and unforeseen additions would have to be built. This is the story told in this volume.

The general prospect ahead was favorable. The industrial revolution unleashed in the previous years rolled resolutely forward through the 1900s. Ahead was a consumer culture that would lead to the highest standard of living ever seen on the face of the globe, along with affluence on the one side and pervasive poverty on the other. The urban concentration started after the Civil War continued. Like much of American life the city would reach an apex during the twentieth century and by the last decades of the century also become the seat of deterioration and violence.

Another fundamental change must be brought into the mix—a change not as obvious as the industrial revolution but none the less as influential, particularly for the public library. This was the steady shift from an oral society to a literate society. Well into the nineteenth century, communication and education were primarily by word of mouth, by means of the spoken word. Then formal schooling spread, more of the people were able to read, and transactions and exchanges took place as much by the written and printed word. A new world opened before a literate population, and the public library would be part of the infrastructure of that new world.

Education had settled into a three-tier system by 1900. The elementary school was widespread, the high school was accepted as a means for those who wanted to press further, and the college and university were the capstones of the system for producing the professionals and specialists needed by the expanding country. Mandatory attendance had appeared. These various units came to have their own libraries, but they needed the public library to supplement their own services and to provide a source of continuing education and information throughout life. The larger literate and educated population that resulted produced more potential users for public libraries.

And the human aspirations that had given birth to the public library—democracy, humanitarianism, literacy—not only prevailed but flourished as the decades went by. The years before had prepared the ground; now the twentieth century would nourish the institution. The American spirit that moved the country from a frontier society to an industrial society in the nineteenth century burned bright into the next years. The people as a whole, with librarians included, were ready for a great surge forward.

Our task here is to trace in general terms the panorama of the twentieth century and to fit the public library in some detail into this historical sequence.

## Notes

1. Edith P. Meyer, *Meet the Future: People and Ideas in the Libraries of Today and Tomorrow*. (Boston: Little, Brown, 1964), 211

2. John S. Brubacher (ed.), *Henry Barnard on Education*. (New York: McGraw-Hill, 1931), 53.

3. Jean B. Molz, "The Reverend Thomas Bray, Pioneer of Libraries" (master's thesis, Drexel Institute of Technology, 1950).

4. Alice C. Dodge, "Origins of the School District Library Movement in New York State (master's thesis, University of Chicago, 1944).

5. Michael H. Harris, *History of Libraries in the Western World*, 4th ed. (Metuchen, N.J.: Scarecrow Press, 1995), 184.

6. William D. Boyd, "Books for Young Businessmen, Mercantile Libraries in the United States, 1820–1865" (Ph.D. diss., Indiana University, 1975).

7. Victoria K. Mussman, "Women and the Founding of Social Libraries in California, 1859–1910." (Ph.D. diss., University of Southern California, 1982).

8. Elfrieda B. McCauley, "The New England Mill Girls: Feminine Influence in the Development of Public Libraries in New England." (Ph.D. diss., Columbia University, 1971).

9. Jesse Shera, *Foundations of the Public Library* (Chicago: University of Chicago Press, 1949), 200–44.

10. U.S. Bureau of Education *Statistics of Libraries and Library Legislation in the United States, 1895–1896*. (Washington, D.C.: Government Printing Office, 1897).

# 2

# The Foundation Years, 1900–1917

For a century, America had been expanding, developing, and diversifying. Democracy had found roots in a settled federal government in forty-five states by 1900, in local councils and school boards—and particularly in the minds of men and women. The year 1900 was more than a statistical turning point. It was a watershed, with a rural community-based life behind it and an urban, industrial, information society before it.

For those of us born in these years, it was to be a time of opportunity. Many started out from humble beginnings (neither of my parents completed elementary school) and halfway through the century were established in the professions, in business, and in technical positions. We saw the bright beginning. We did not foresee wars hot and cold, or depression, or violence and terrorism, or the widespread alienation and cynicism that would mark the end of the century.

By 1900 large-scale corporations had come into existence: Standard Oil under John D. Rockefeller, American Telephone and Telegraph under Theodore Vail, and—not least for our purpose—United States Steel under Andrew Carnegie. Henry Ford produced his first automobiles for general purchase ($680) in 1908 and he designed the assembly line in 1913. In 1906 the Wright brothers flew an airborne contrivance 852 feet; by the end of the century the Concorde flew across the Atlantic Ocean at 1,000 miles per hour. "National Wealth, income and the output of manufacturing more than doubled in the first twelve years of the century."[1]

Large cities grew larger, gathering in families from the countryside and from Europe. The city would be the fulcrum for business, manufacturing, art and entertainment,—and for large public libraries for the next many decades. Immigration reached a peak in the first and second decades, up to the time of legal limits enacted in 1924. Europeans poured into what they saw as the promised land, and with their desire for freedom and with their family values to sustain them, many would realize the promise. The United States would finally reach a summit and by the later years of the century sought ways to cut off the flow of foreigners.

Communication was burgeoning at the beginning of the century. You could pick up the telephone and talk to someone at a distance, turn on the phonograph and listen to Caruso, go to one of the first movies or listen to one of the first radio programs, even take a photograph to recall an incident at a later time. Electricity had come to the city, so that one did not have far to go to plug in these various devices. Skyscrapers appeared in New York and Chicago. Until World War I it was a time of enterprise and optimism.

New ideas flowed in through the marvelous medium of books. Thoughtful people were digesting the contrary ideas in *The Education of Henry Adams* (1907), in which the author projects the disturbing image of the "dynamo" as predicting the next years. Then there were Sigmund Freud and John Dewey to be understood and Mark Twain and Willa Cather to be enjoyed. People were trying to grasp fresh ideas: evolution, pragmatism, Oedipus complex, relativity. Even in these early years one can discern the seeds of discontent appearing first in the literature of the times. Lincoln Steffens produced *The Shame of Cities* (1904), Upton Sinclair *The Jungle* (1906), and Frank Norris *The Pit* (1903). In summarizing later decades we will again note that realistic authors often pointed first to deep-rooted problems just coming to the surface.

Theodore Roosevelt and Woodrow Wilson were the dominant presidential figures of the period, very different individuals but each with a vision of the nation. Both received the Nobel Peace Prize.

Roosevelt pushed hard for legislation strengthening the position of the common man and furthering the conservation of national resources, and he put the United States squarely on the world stage. Under him the Panama Canal was completed. He nourished the upbeat and constructive spirit of the times.

Wilson, a more reflective person, pushed through tariff reform, the control of monopolies, and improvement in the banking system. He was reelected in 1916 on the promise that he would keep the United States out of the war spreading in Europe. However, with the sinking of the Lusitania (1,198 lives lost) and the ruthless submarine warfare, we were drawn in.

Starting with an assassination in Sarajevo in Bosnia, World War I soon involved most of the countries of Europe, and in time settled down into three years of trench warfare along a 450-mile front. Civilian populations were affected by air raids and poison-gas attacks. The United States sent two million men into the conflict, and suffered 375,000 casualties with 115,000 dead.

In the end, Wilson held to the high road: in the peace conference he presented Fourteen Points "to make the world safe for democracy," which the Allied leaders diluted point by point, and he pushed for a League of Nations which the U.S. Senate rejected. Shattered in health, his office in his last year in the White House was actually run by his wife.

In these swirling events, how did the public library fare?

## Overview of Library Development, 1900–1917

By 1900 there were approximately two thousand public libraries in the United States.[2] By 1918 the figure was close to six thousand. The idea was catching on. These were the founding years when the base of the structure came into place.

Most of the larger cities had an agency by the turn of the century. Eighty percent of the 137 cities in the country with a population over thirty thousand had a public library. In the first two decades of the century most of the rest fell into line. The percentage of municipalities under thirty thousand in population that had a library was not as high, but a majority of cities had taken the step before World War I. Statistics prove most of the libraries started in these early years were in relatively small centers (which created a problem that led to a later move for larger units of service—see the 1931–45 period).

As to why the public library flourished with the new century, no doubt the same forces that brought subscription libraries into existence in the nineteenth century continued to apply in the twentieth. A whole people reached for its destiny, and education was among the most important means for doing so. This was not solely a movement for educating children; lyceums, Chautauquas, and discussion groups sprouted. Adults wanted to know, to understand, to experience vicariously. In addition, there was just the pleasure of using the ability to read, almost like finding a new food source, and this applied whether the material read was Francis Parkman on the growth of America before the revolution or a throwaway romance by Gene Stratton Porter. There may even have been some element of "keeping up with the Joneses" at work here; a community might want a public library as a kind of badge of culture.

This is not to say that all the new libraries were vital, expanding agencies. Some were on a side street, both physically and socially, ignored by the bulk of the population and passed over by public officials at budget time. Most of these weak, uncertain beginnings went unrecorded and are now past history. When more careful attention is directed to the early years, the slow beginnings appear in the record. For example, the Akron, Ohio public library struggled for decades until receiving help from the Works Progress Administration in the 1930s.[3]

But sturdy growth mostly occurred in the early years of the century. They could be called the "missionary" years. In city after city missionaries stood up and preached the doctrine. These were able, dedicated administrators, both men and women (brief biographies of the more prominent among them will be presented after describing the institution they brought into place). Their message reached not only the general public, who became users of the library, but also public officials who provided it with funds.

The mission of the growing institution will be examined first and then the Carnegie grants, one of the main sources of the surge forward in the early 1900s. Then comes discussion of the governmental structure of the agency, followed by a description of its basic characteristics: direct access to resources, types of materials organized for use, and nearby locations by means of branches. These efforts will continue throughout the century, so that the public library put into place by the 1910s differs little from today's facility.

## The Mission of the Public Library

One searches in vain in the professional literature of these early years for any explicit mention of concern about the goals and objectives of the public library. This was true of annual reports of libraries, records of proceedings at professional meetings, as well as journal articles. Objectives were assumed by librarians to be self-evident; there was no need to hold them up to scrutiny.

There were three assumed objectives. The oldest was articulated by the moving spirits of the public library, such as George Ticknor and Edward Everett at the opening of the Boston Public Library in 1854. It was to provide a record of knowledge, a collection of the classics and subject publications which were the common heritage of educated adults. The second purpose, not prominent until later in the century, was to support the widespread self-education movement in which segments of the population examined at least part of the record of knowledge. The third appearing late in the nineteenth century, in response to a great spurt in the publishing of popular material in America, led to the provision of recreational reading, what was referred to as "wholesome recreation."

The earlier emphasis upon a record of the world of knowledge can be called the humanitarian view of the mission of the institution. It was an elitist conception of what people ought to read. We will shortly see this trend picked up by revisionist historians to derive a reform motive for establishing the public library.

The later emphasis upon education and wholesome recreation can properly be called a democratic view of the purpose of the public library. The humanitarian view was imposed from above; the democratic conception came from the people, the culmination of the many social libraries of the nineteenth century that led in time to the twentieth century institution which we now know.

The humanitarian strain pointed toward collections made up of classics, approved literary works, and standard subject books. The educational goal required publications that specifically supported the self-improvement activities in which people were engaged. And the recreational aim called for the popular current literature designed to provide diversion. The three pulled in different directions and competed for the limited money available.

In seeking to identify the mission of the public library at the opening of the twentieth century, it helps to look back briefly at the founding years in the mid-nineteenth century. Three historical students of note dug into the earlier record: Jesse Shera, Robert Lee, and Sidney Ditzion.

Taking Ditzion first,[4] he sought to relate the emerging institution to its cultural setting and to the social changes occurring in the second half of the nineteenth century. He emphasizes the democratic strivings of the period. In his view, it was citizenship and the desire for "informed voters" that motivated both the general public and governmental officials to support the stripling agency[5]—thus his title, *Arsenals of a Democratic Culture.*

Robert Lee stresses more the educational rationale for the public library.[6] Quoting extensively from Edward Everett, one of the founders of the Boston Public Library, he states, "The first principles of popular government require that the means of education should . . . be equally within reach of the whole population." Lee sees the public library as an extension of the public schools, providing what he calls "continuing education." It is worth noting the altruistic and optimistic viewpoint reflected in the interpretations by both Ditzion and Lee. They assumed that "the whole population" would have the incentive to continue education and cultural growth, which was not true either in that day or this.

Jesse Shera probed deeper in his landmark history of the public library in the early years.[7] He analyzed the books actually provided in the newly emerging public libraries and describes them as "titles that more properly belonged in the study of the man of letters." Shera pushed his interpretation further and questioned the relevance of libraries as educators. To him, the educator is a leader who conducts students into the unknown: "The librarian by the very nature of the responsibilities which he has assumed cannot function effectively as such a leader."[8] Then he gets carried away: "To reason that because educators and librarians both make use of books and ideas are educators is equivalent to saying Old Dutch Cleanser is a food merely because it is usually kept in the kitchen and used by the cook."[9] Leaving the cleanser on the shelf for the moment, Shera persists in his view. He refers to the "unrealistic infatuation of the librarian with his educational responsibilities." Involved here is the question of the definition of "education" that is used. The question of definition recurs when we look at the later revisionist interpretations of the role of the public library.

More recent interpreters have taken up the controversy, individuals who can be called revisionist historians. Dee Garrison concluded that "the building of public libraries was motivated by a fear of egalitarianism and upheaval from below as much as by a desire for democratic extension of education."[10] She also believed that "the public library . . . was chiefly concerned with arresting change in literary and moral standards."[11] The author supports this position by an analysis of the social backgrounds, personal values and published writings of leading librarians, particularly scholarly Justin Winsor, hearty William Poole, and systematic Charles Cutter, the three men who served as presidents of the American Library Association from 1876 to 1888. Put colloquially, the public library was seen by the conservatives as a rival to the saloon. By the end of the nineteenth century fresh voices came forward in the persons of Melvil Dewey, the organizer, and John Cotton Dana, the challenger, and the democratic mission gained control.

Later, in the 1970s, Michael Harris took up the revisionist position concerning the early years of the public library. The proponents of the Boston Public Library and others, he noted, were upper-class, well-educated individuals. His interpretation was that their motives were not so much to liberate the mass of people but rather to control the masses because of fear of unrest and revolt.[12] This provoked a response from Phyllis Dain, who cited lack of evidence for the revisionist position.[13]

If the "gentry" sought to control the rebellious elements in society by means of the public library, it was a forlorn hope. Most of the library users did not come from the ranks of manual workers and labor union members, nor from families of limited education, but from more established members of society—indeed, from persons similar in outlook to the gentry themselves.

The revisionist view in history can often penetrate below the polite surface of sanctified beliefs, but this view can also get caught up in its own rhetoric and enthusiasm. Consider this evaluation of the public library as of 1920: "The public library survived as a peripheral cultural and intellectual institution, chiefly providing light fiction to middle-class women and children, encased in an image of genteel traditionalism, ineffectual males and shushing spinsters."[14] This judgment was made just as the public library was about to surge forward with a variety of reader services.

The lesson in these various exchanges is that the public library had mixed purposes from the beginning, humanitarian on the one side and democratic on the other. By the new century the democratic aims of popular education and wholesome recreation were in the saddle; the elitist view had fallen back but remained in the habitual practice of also providing the classics and the historical volumes of a gentleman's library.

In considering these various views, traditional and revisionist, it is worth remembering that it is possible to draw too sharp a line between these several purposes. One of the marvels of a book is that it can serve more than one aim at a time. A reader picks up a novel for diversion, to fill a quiet evening after turning off the television, yet he or she may gain understanding of human nature in the process, or may gain insight into the historical period in which the story is set (*Northwest Passage, Drums Along the Mohawk, My Antonia*). Conversely, other readers may pick up a volume on astronomy or gardening not solely for understanding but also for diversion, because this is the way they relax. Or individuals may seek out material for a foreign affairs discussion group and end up studying the history and literature of an unfamiliar country. From pure diversion on the one side to concentrated study on the other, there is a seamless web that defies convenient labels. This is the fascinating interface between human nature, in all its diversity, and the world of books, with all its variety.

As this history proceeds we will see various additions to the purposes of the public library: an information source, personal guidance in reading for children, for teenagers, and for adults; business service; Americanization; book reviews and book discussions; community center; a storehouse for older, local records.

All things to all people. Throughout this story we will note the interplay among these various programs and the rise and fall of some of them.

At the turn of the century, the controversial views came to be embodied in what was termed the "fiction problem." In the late decades of the nineteenth century, romantic novels had become popular. Some critics, including some librarians, considered them not only to be of questionable literary value but, more serious, judged them to be "immoral." Two viewpoints contested with each other in the earlier decades: one view rejected current fiction because it did not meet standards and the other accepted this material on the grounds that it would attract additional readers who would later go on to more substantial (respectable) publications. The latter position won out, even though it was never proven to be true. As the Victorian ethos declined and as fresh voices were raised in librarianship, the judgmental position was put aside well before World War I. Popular fiction came to be included in public library collections as the agency sought to serve a wider segment of the population.

Putting the several pieces together, was the public library in the early years of the century just a free bookstore? What was special about this institution? What prompted government to underwrite this public interest and not other interests of the populace such as health or entertainment or sports? The answer was that the general public and the elected officials—then and now—pictured it as an educational agency, there to help people to understand the world, to prepare them to function as citizens, and to gain information needed for their employment and their daily tasks. And education had come to be an accepted public responsibility. There were the elementary schools for the basic schooling of children and the emerging secondary schools; the public library would pick up the mission and become what was later called the People's University. Officialdom discerned a purpose not yet clearly articulated by librarians—indeed librarians at first tended more to concentrate upon the other two strands, the basic subject collection and recreational reading.

Several decades passed before administrators stood back, appraised the situation, and established goals. Later in the century we will note voices raised urging priorities and concentration, but even today there are not many libraries that have adopted mission statements. We are dealing with a multipurpose agency, and this multiplicity of aims will affect progress in every stage of this history—indeed will limit effectiveness of the library at various points.

The public library continued on through the first half of the century with its many-sided programs. Different purposes were later brought into the picture.

No matter what the mixture of the two strands, humanitarian and democratic, at the beginning of the century, the latter came to dominate in the succeeding decades, to make the popular, people-oriented institution which we know today. The concept of democracy, in all its ramifications, contributed to the growth of the library. Progress was in the air. Getting ahead was a shared goal. Government by the people flourished. The public library, it was felt, would help achieve each of these goals. This volume's task is to determine the extent to which these various goals were actually realized.

## The Carnegie Buildings

Andrew Carnegie was a driven man: driven in building up his fortune, then driven in giving it away, to the amount of $310 million, including grants to construct 1,679 libraries. He was a ruthless business competitor in building the Carnegie Steel Company. He was equally ambitious in all walks of life; he was not satisfied on the golf course unless he beat each of his fellow golfers.

In his advanced years, Carnegie wrote a series of essays on the responsibilities of the rich to help the poor. One essay was titled "The Advantages of Poverty."[15] The advantage was that it developed the character and the drive to succeed. Noble sentiments were expressed throughout his writings: "The problem of our age is the proper administration of wealth, that the ties of brotherhood may still bind together the rich and poor in harmonious relationships."[16] A remarkable and complex man, Carnegie was an individual worthy of a major biography, which fortunately has been written.[17] A more recent book by Abigail Van Slyck probes deeper into the architectural impact of the Carnegie buildings.

A self-made millionaire, Andrew Carnegie saw in the public

library an agency that would enable others to follow in his footsteps. Not formal education, not classes and credits, he put his money on individual initiative and personal study to grow and advance. Here was an agency that had developed throughout his lifetime and that had great potential. He said: "I chose free libraries as the best agencies for improving the masses of the people, because they only help those who help themselves. They reach the aspiring, and open to these the chief treasures of the world."

The Carnegie grants came at just the right time. As we have seen, by 1900 almost two thousand public libraries existed in the United States. Carnegie's money doubled that figure by World War I. An institution that was gaining public recognition had found its champion.

The first grants were made to communities in western Pennsylvania where the Carnegie Steel Company had been concentrated: Pittsburgh, Allegheny, Johnstown, Braddock, Homestead. Large grants were made to New York City and to Philadelphia for branch libraries, which Andrew Carnegie favored because they were local and close to the people. Many requests from the Midwest were granted and relatively few were received from the Southeast and Southwest.[19]

There were two essential requirements to get a grant: that a site be provided for the building, and that the locality commit itself to provide at least 10 percent of the grant for annual maintenance. The commitment came from municipal officials, not solely from the librarian or the library board. At first no review of physical plans for the proposed structures were required, but after 1908 such information had to be submitted and was reviewed, usually by James Bertram, Carnegie's secretary. In smaller structures a layout was favored that provided two levels, the collection and reading rooms on the main floor—circulation desk before the entrance and reading rooms for adults and for children to each side—and utilities and storage in the basement, perhaps with an assembly or lecture room. A half-dozen steps led up to the dignified entrance. Local architects were used, but they learned to take a look at other Carnegie buildings, so that many of the smaller structures took on a characteristic appearance; one can still occasionally note a Carnegie library in driving through a locality, even though the building may no longer be used for library purposes. A recent reappraisal notes that while all Carnegie buildings were designed locally they all gave a sense of being alike.[20]

The size of grants differed widely. A fair number were under $10,000, while several cities received more than a million dollars (New York, Philadelphia and Pittsburgh). Medium-sized cities received substantial grants (Cleveland $590,000, Cincinnati $286,000, Denver $360,000, Detroit $750,000, Seattle $430,000). At times stipends were reduced when cities would not guarantee the 10 percent annual support.

It would be heartening to be able to report that all the grants for libraries were received with gratitude by all elements in the population, and heartening also to report that all recipients proceeded to maintain strong and effective agencies. However, this is not the case. There was opposition based on the source of the Carnegie money, right down to the deaths at the Homestead strike. Some localities failed to live up to their pledge of providing annual support equal to 10 percent of the grant received. Most serious was the criticism that no money was provided for books: some buildings opened with only a few books on the shelves and a few had to postpone opening (Tampa, Florida, for example) until they could accumulate the beginning of a collection.

But there can be little doubt that the Carnegie building grants gave a boost to the public-library movement at a strategic stage. Libraries appeared across the land. More than that, local governments came to accept libraries as part of their responsibility. The Carnegie buildings raised the esteem with which libraries were held, which in turn led to the financial support which initiated the new, innovative services of the 1920s.

The most thorough chronicle of the Carnegie gifts and buildings sees the early grants as a stimulus that carried forward, with later Carnegie Corporation money, to the reorganization of education for library service, to the creation of national standards, to the Public Library Inquiry of 1950, and culminating in the national Libraries Service and Construction Act of 1964. "Carnegie's benefactions have, in truth, played a major role in American public library development."[21]

## The Government of the Library

As public libraries were established in the nineteenth and early twentieth centuries, there were several possible alternatives for their governmental organization. Here were the main possibilities:

1. Create another division of local government, similar to a police or fire department, or a street maintenance or health department.
2. Create a division within an existing department, such as a section under a human services department or a section under a schools department.
3. Create a self-governing division under an elected board of directors, such as a board of education.
4. Create a self-governing division under an appointed board of directors.

The choice selected would have significance for the development and future of the agency. If a regular department or division status were chosen, directly under the local governing body and directly under the local administrative officer (mayor or city manager), the library would be close to the center of local government, with direct access in presenting its needs and problems. On the other hand, it would be immediately subject to political and policy pressures. If, on the contrary, it were to function under an elected board, the library would itself be in the political arena, with individuals and groups competing to gain control, as in some boards of education.

The alternative that came to prevail was control under an appointed board. Why was this governmental form chosen? Because it was a natural extension of the form that the predecessors of the agency had followed in the nineteenth century. Most of the social and subscription libraries were started by interested individuals who then came to constitute a controlling policy body in one form or another. If development by committed individuals had brought the institution to its promising stage by 1900, why not continue the pattern? The government of the Boston Public Library, established in 1854, reflected this same model, with individuals such as Edward Everett and George Ticknor strongly influencing the purpose and structure of this early agency.

This does not mean that public libraries founded before and after 1900 were independent of local government. If they were, they were not public libraries by the definition that we have adopted. Actually, the agencies that emerged in the nineteenth century and then in the twentieth were units of local government. The city or town or county still controlled who was appointed to the library board and also controlled financial support (over and above endowments and financial gifts). The local government controlled the purse strings; the local government alone had the authority to issue bonds to finance the construction of buildings.

Actually, this particular form was not selected by the local (city, town, or county) government. Public libraries are organized under state law. The locality, once it decided to establish a library, had little choice as to structure, for the sponsors of library development had turned to the next higher level of government. State library agencies had appeared in the nineteenth century, with both collections in support of state government and units devoted to establishment and extension of agencies over the state. The individual library advocates and the extension people got together and jointly pushed their campaigns. The government offices got legislation passed specifying the form of local control under appointed boards. Thus all the sponsors—state, local, and individual—pushed together and this accounted for the many public libraries established in the first years of the century.

Carleton Joeckel tells this story in one of the distinguished publications in the library field, his *Government of the Public Library* (University of Chicago Press, 1935). It is a story to warm the hearts not only of those who love books and reading but also those who believe that individual volunteer effort can build institutions. Present-day reformers who believe that the need now in the face of big government is the upswelling of local initiative and the creation of grassroots institutions would do well to look back at the beginning of the public library.

Legislation in most of the states specifies the structure of local library government, number of members on the board, terms of office, and legal prerogatives. This is done under the rubric of the American constitutional system which places responsibility for education at the state level (that is, does not specify education at the federal level and therefore leaves it to the states).

The New Jersey law is typical:

> The Board shall hold in trust and manage all property of the Library. It may rent rooms, or, when proper, construct buildings for

> the use of the library, purchase books, pamphlets, documents, papers and other reading matter, hire librarians and other necessary personnel, and fix their compensation, make proper rules and regulations for the government of the library, and generally do all things necessary and proper for the establishment and maintenance of the free public library in the municipality.[23]

This covers the waterfront. The board clearly has complete control. Citizens appointed to library boards, who may have thought that they would simply express opinions about books and service programs when asked, are often surprised at the scope of their legal responsibility. Legislation differs in details from state to state, but this is the usual pattern.

Not all public libraries follow this local-appointed board pattern. In a small percentage of cities—some in California, for example—the agency operates as a regular department directly under the city manager. Also, in a few jurisdictions, library board members are elected rather than appointed, Minneapolis and Grand Rapids being examples. In an even smaller percentage the library is governed by a self-perpetuating board, a carryover from past history.

The predominant board form has over the years brought forth a goodly number of genuine civic leaders devoted to the institution. The appointed trustees, serving without compensation and often without visible recognition, have often worked hard in the cause, raised funds as necessary, resisted efforts of special-interest groups to influence the content of collections, and stepped in when an internal crisis appeared. All communities have at least a small number of civic-minded leaders who avoid elective office but welcome a connection with a respected agency such as the public library. A roster of these unsung heroes and heroines would bulk large among outstanding citizens in American life.

The board form of library government has not been without faults and shortcomings. There have been many passive members who have dutifully attended meetings, nodded in agreement when action was proposed, and sat mute when trouble was encountered. On the other side there have been some who tried to muscle in on the territory of the hired director and staff. Some have clung to board membership over the decades and even over generations, even though state law may specify limited terms of office.

A continuing issue has been the limits of authority of the library board of directors on the one side and the local government on the other. Once appointed, the trustees have responsibility under state law to determine policy, to appoint a director of the agency, to control finances, and even in some cases to "approve" book selection. But what if the local government decrees a 5 percent cut in salary for municipal employees or simply an extra holiday when governmental units will be closed. Is the library required to follow suit—whose authority will prevail? Such questions arose at the beginning of the century and they have continued through the years. Often the library board decides to go along with such dictates in the interest of preserving smooth relations with the funding source. Where the board has resisted and the question has gone to adjudication, the decision may fall on one side or the other, so that to this day this is an uncertain area. Alex Ladenson's *American Library Laws*, has analyzed the question in greater detail.

On balance, the board form of government has been an asset and deserves some of the credit for the success of the institution. At times it has called forth leadership in the ranks of trustees. Boards have usually supported the actions of their chief librarians. As we will see when considering efforts to slant collections in one direction or another, they have resisted attempts at censorship. The appointed board form of library government has channeled positive community support into this civic educational agency. It will be a guiding light and an anchor to windward as the public library determines its role in the twenty-first century.

By 1900, twenty-nine of the (then) forty-five states had passed legislation authorizing local public libraries, and the remaining states followed soon after. In general, the pattern was as indicated above, with particular twists in one or another state. There has been no movement throughout the twentieth century to change the governmental base of the public library.

## Open Access to Resources

A long tradition in library administration, going back several centuries, accepted closed shelves without review or appraisal. The reader submitted a request and an attendant went to the closed shelves and produced the book requested. By this means damage to materials was prevented, books were not misused, nor were they stolen. Also, mixing up the arrangement of items on the shelves by users was avoided, so that time and effort were not needed to straighten out the collection. The preservation function was stressed.

Looking back now, one is surprised to note that this practice was widely accepted not just in university and scholarly collections, but also in public libraries, right up to 1900. Small collections might be open but not the more substantial holdings in larger agencies. Arthur E. Bostwick notes that "In a discussion of free access in the Conference of Libraries held in London, October 2–5, 1877, at which many Americans were present, the majority of those who spoke, including Dr. Melvil Dewey, condemned it."[24]

Twenty-five years later, at the beginning of the twentieth century, a debate reported in the *Library Journal* came to the same conclusion. The view of one of the participants was expressed with feeling:

> Order is heaven's first law, and above all things in a library. Where "go and help yourself" is the rule, where a hundred or more men, woman and children are roaming around, taking down book after book to see how it looks inside, you may possibly find the book you want, but the chances are against you and the assistants are as helpless.[25]

A staff member assigned the task of straightening the shelves today might well sympathize with this view.

Many libraries did make small collections of certain books openly available. This applied at first to standard reference books and then gradually spread to other categories. Oddly enough, for some time restricted access was retained for fiction books (because some had immoral passages), including some of the classics, and even children's books. It was feared that youngsters would misuse them.

The Cleveland Public Library broke with the tradition in 1890 and the Free Library of Philadelphia in 1895. Reports back from such sources stated, surprisingly enough, that materials were not being misused or lost; that in fact use had increased. Other public libraries tried open access to at least part of the collection and then to most other materials. Slowly, but steadily, the objections to open shelves were discounted, counterbalanced by the advantage of greater use. The reader-oriented library was winning out over the preservation-oriented library. By the time of the increase in Carnegie building grants, a little later in the first decade of the century, open access was usually taken for granted. There were a few libraries that pulled back after opening the shelves, but these were infrequent. There were a few holdouts; the Enoch Pratt Free Library, which was to become an innovator in the 1930s and beyond, actually kept closed shelves until the 1920s. But one after another, public libraries, large and small, made the change. A practice in keeping with the people's and community nature of the public library had prevailed. The materials belonged to the people; they should have access to them.

Significant in itself, the opening of access directly to books on the shelves was symbolic of the emerging institutions. It took a basic change of attitude on the part of librarians to bring about this change. This was to be the people's library, as distinct from the scholar's library. It was to be responsive to all sections of the public, to the casual reader as well as the serious student, to the follower of ancient history as well as the person interested in yesterday's stock prices, to those who liked Shakespeare and to those who preferred Jack London.

Today, we consider this attitude admirable. At the same time it prepared the way for a multisided institution, for a multipurpose agency, sometimes pulled in different directions. It prepared the way for a service that at times had ambitions beyond its capacities. We will note the consequences of this attitude throughout this history.

## Collections Organized for Use

The very fact of a gathering of books and other media—a collection—opens a great opportunity to users. A wide swath of knowledge has been captured. Even a collection of only a few thousand volumes acquired by a library in 1900 or 1910 opened vistas available, without the agency, to only a few of the richest of individuals. The gathering alone is significant.

But how will users find the particular material they need, how will they gain access to the accumulated power? The answer is in the further step that librarians take. They organize the collection for use. This step is important, because it calls on a high degree of organizational and literary skill. Anyone lost today on the Internet would appreciate organization for use.

But what basis of organization is to be used? In the nineteenth century, many libraries used a system of "fixed location." Each volume was assigned a serial number as it arrived and this number determined its location on the shelves. But of course acquisitions did not arrive in subject groupings. Fixed locations meant that the first book acquired on a given topic would stand near the beginning and the last near the end, with others scattered in between. This was acceptable as long as shelves were not open to the public, for the user looked in a catalog, got the serial number of the item desired, and an attendant got it from its fixed location. But obviously this plan offered no logical grouping or order once open shelves were adopted.

Over the years, the philosophical challenge of the division and classification of knowledge intrigued scholars, back to Francis Bacon's scheme put forth in 1605. Many other plans came out of the scholar's study in the seventeenth and eighteenth centuries. Growing library collections called forth fresh efforts, directed to the practical purpose of arranging publications so they could be readily located and at the same time would be grouped so that similar items could be examined and compared. A further requirement was that the system be expansive in order to accommodate new subjects as they appeared. Standing out among these was W. P. Cutter's Expansive Classification of 1897. He classified topics by letters and combinations of letters, plus numbers for expansion, an approach which was used in the Library of Congress classification.

However, users of public libraries could not readily comprehend the more complicated schemes. What was needed was a relatively simple plan which both staff and readers could keep in mind, and which still had provision for subdivision and expansion. Such an arrangement could be taught to young students and hopefully they could continue to use it in later years.

Before 1900, a wide range of classification plans were used in public libraries, often, improvisations—home grown schemes—

thought up by local personnel. Smaller collections might simply be arranged by broad categories that readily come to mind—novels, biography, history, science, practical arts—with shelf labels to identify each. There was no overall rationale or system for the plan, and inevitably a considerable batch of miscellaneous titles would accumulate. It was not easy to explain the plan either to students or adults.

Quite early the fiction—nonfiction distinction was adopted. This was before novels about actual events became fairly common. For example, good introductions to early American history are Kenneth Robert's *Northwest Passage* and Walter Edmond's *Drums Along the Mohawk*, or for more recent events Norman Mailer's *The Naked and the Dead*. Or for insight into human nature, a reader could do worse than start with some of the classics, whether *The Scarlet Letter* or *The Brothers Karamazov*. All of these titles sit on the fiction shelves among romances and mysteries. The separation of fiction and nonfiction is of course maintained to this day, despite the many crossovers. In the minds not only of readers, but also of some librarians, there is a problem with the Literature section of the nonfiction category: do Shakespeare's words go in the 800s (Literature) or in fiction?

Also fairly early it was recognized that some works are intended for short-term consultation and not for extended reading at home, so the separate "reference" shelves were set up. This distinction has also been widely adopted and is still maintained. The distinction is not always clear to users. To begin with, the term "reference" is not self-explanatory: refer to what or to whom? On which side does a book of menus for meals belong, or an explanation of computer terms? Some librarians have added to the confusion by using the reference, no-circulation shelves for valuable art books or specially-illustrated material.

Melvil Dewey invented his decimal classification system in 1876. By 1900 it had been widely adopted by public libraries and was uniformly adopted by the additional agencies set up in the first years of the century. The system divided knowledge into ten categories, and then subdivided each category into ten subunits, and each subunit in turn into ten individual numbers for different topics. By adding a decimal point, each topic could be divided further. Some numbers became rather complicated—973.9217, for example—and even librarians may not be sure of the meaning of the numbers after the decimal point. By and large the whole system has held up quite well, although rapidly developing areas such as medicine and computers do not have enough subdivisions because of recent developments. This is not a foolproof system, but it was a stroke of genius. Few users of libraries could pass a test on the Dewey decimal system, although many do get a sense of the broad plan, and they come to remember the particular numbers of special interest to them. For librarians the Dewey plan gives them a sense of overall organization and enables them to find their way to individual subjects.

As in any one-dimensional classification system, individual publications can be placed in more than one location in the plan. An example would be a volume on the Erie Canal in upstate New York, with some description and history; it could go in 368 on canals . . . or in 917.4 with other material on geography and travel, or in 973.4 on the history of the Middle Atlantic states. These are quite separate locations in the overall scheme. One can only depend on the judgment of the librarian on the job as to the best location (that is, the location more likely to serve the particular clientele of the library), and also on the related catalog that brings together the various publications on the Erie Canal. Searchers can turn to numbers with which they are familiar, or—better yet—can consult the catalog and get an exact location number. As early as the 1900s many public libraries provided for this double-track approach.

A library is more than a collection; it is an *organized* collection. This is a significant aid and guide for users. By the turn of the century, readers came to expect and depend upon the organization. They would have been surprised and confused if 10,000 volumes or 100,000 volumes were scattered helter-skelter on the shelves or grouped under a few broad categories.

Also by 1900 the card catalog was widespread. Being alphabetical in arrangement and each card representing one volume, the card catalog was not difficult to use. It informed the searcher as to whether a library possessed a particular item or material on a particular subject, and also provided a location number. Even elementary level students learned to use the card catalog, and even oldsters set in their ways had little trouble with it.

The Library of Congress began printing catalog cards for distribution in 1902, and the H. W. Wilson and Bowker companies not long after. Individual libraries could purchase the cards in sets for the titles they acquired, getting not just the cards themselves, but also the expertise that had gone into the bibliographical description of the item. Users now had a fairly uniform tool and index with which they were familiar, like a dictionary or an encyclopedia.

As early as the first decades of the century, public libraries were organized for use, not a small accomplishment. At the same time it would be overly sanguine to say that everyone found his or her way easily in them, either then or now. Help and guidance were still needed, and came into the picture in the next period of the 1920s.

## Extension and Branches

As part of the burgeoning of the institution before World War I, attention was given to bringing library service close to people. The goal was to have not just the collection in the center of the city, but also branches in the neighborhoods, not just the library in a distant center, but also mobile units coming out to readers. Small collections were even packaged, and left for considerable periods in local stores, in schools, in churches, even individual homes that were then opened to neighbors.

All this effort resulted from recognition that convenience was a definite factor in whether people read or not. The underlying motivation was to reach casual readers. Individuals with a compelling purpose would typically travel a considerable distance to get what they needed, but someone looking for "something to read" would find other diversions unless the circulating collection turned up nearby. This emphasis on convenience and extension, distinguishes, the American public library from some of its European counterparts, even to this day.

The early public libraries were established in cities. Between cities there were vast stretches of rural areas, particularly at the turn of the century, and most of them were without a public source of books unless the farmer hitched up the team and made the long trip into the city. Even when arriving there he and his family were often turned down for borrowing privileges at the public library, unless he paid a special nonresident fee.

The state level stepped into this gap. Extension divisions were organized with primary responsibility for rural readers. Sometimes the unit was a department within the state libraries that had been created to provide resources for the state legislature and state departments. Occasionally the unit was a division within the department of education. Most frequently it was a new and independent agency, the state library commission. No particular advantage can be reported for any one of the three; each was likely to be animated by a spirit of extension to cover as much of the state as possible. However, in reality, different states had varying degrees of success in achieving this goal, depending on the money and effort expended and on circumstances faced, such as the density of population: New York State, for example, brought library service to most of its area more rapidly than Nebraska or Texas.

In promoting statewide services, the state agencies in the early 1900s used a variety of tactics. One was simply to send extension agents into unserved areas to arouse interest and to offer help in getting started. Another was to deposit small collections of books in unserved localities, hoping thereby to stimulate local action. Mobile units were used for the same purpose. At first horse-drawn vehicles and later early versions of bookmobiles were used. More formal demonstrations were occasionally set up, as in Louisiana, with the intention that the local county (parish) would take over in time. Whenever response became evident, extension workers stood ready to advise and help. And the state library collection served as a backup for limited local collections, with material available on interlibrary loan.

The mobile unit going out from the center was the plan adopted most frequently. Looking back from the current period of sleek and well-organized bookmobiles, one needs a bit of imagination to picture Mary Titcomb alone on the driver's seat of the first horse-and-wagon book vehicle, going from town-to-town in Maryland and stopping along the way at rural crossroads and in schoolyards. That was in 1908. But pictures of local people, adults, and children, poring through the books on the side of the wagon and kneeling inside to look at more titles is a symbol of the missionary spirit that animated this early period. The idea caught on in the county libraries that were forming at this time. By the 1920s Traveling Libraries existed even in large cities—in

New York City and in the Richmond borough starting in 1922 and in the Bronx in 1928, for example.

The bookmobile of today carries up to three thousand titles, arranged neatly on shelves, including an encyclopedia and a few dictionaries, and with a small counter for the library attendant, in substance a miniature library on wheels. In another version a trailer truck is used, increasing the capacity and opening the possibility of leaving the vehicle in one location for several days. Convenience and nearby access are the watchwords.

Over the years, as the ownership of automobiles increased and people were able to get to nearby centers, the use of bookmobiles declined to some extent. However, they are still found both in county and city agencies, going out to hamlets and to corners in the city. Some people will pick up a book if it is available down the block, although they will not travel a mile to a branch collection.

As concentrations of population grew up in outlying areas of cities and in counties, what may be called partial branches appeared. These usually took the form of deposit stations where small temporary collections were located. The location might be in a corner of a public building, in a church, or in a fire station. Staffing was provided by whatever personnel was available at the location. Usually local users were encouraged to request special materials they needed from the central collection. Again we see the public library seeking to get close to people.

Complete branch libraries appeared in the outlying neighborhoods of cities in the early 1900s. Not just convenience motivated such extension of service, but a related purpose was to fashion specific programs directly fitting the needs and character of different communities. For example, in Chicago the program needed in the steel mill area of South Chicago was different from that suited to the upper-income area of the North Shore; in New York City, requirements of a neighborhood unit on the Lower East Side were different from those several miles north on the Upper East Side. Whether branches achieved the needed distinctions is a matter of opinion; after a period most of them seemed to fall into a common pattern, with the same fiction titles on the shelves, the same basic nonfiction items, and a children's section.

Branches usually started out rather small, a few thousand volumes and a staff of two or three individuals. They might be located in modest storefront locations in rented quarters or in one room in the fieldhouse of a public park. The distance between units was often less than a mile.

But the concept was sound, local people responded, and pressure was on for expansion. The storefront locations became larger, the fieldhouse locations in time were abandoned, and separate buildings were constructed. Andrew Carnegie gave New York City $5 million to build thirty-nine branches. Today there are over 6,700 branches of city and county libraries in the United States.

Demand increased to the point where some cities developed a new, intermediate level of service. Cleveland and Chicago established regional branches by the 1920s, and other cities later. At this level collections numbered as much as fifty thousand volumes and services included specialized reference and reading guidance. Thus three levels of facility had developed: neighborhood, regional, and central. Indeed branches for specialized subject areas and specialized clienteles appeared for children, business people, and for the study of art and the theater. Adding the several thousand city libraries, the many branches and the occasional county libraries together, over 75 million United States residents had local, accessible library services by 1920, two-thirds of the total population—a remarkable accomplishment. The remaining 35 million would be aimed at in the move for county libraries and larger units of service in the following two decades.

## The American Library Association

The American Library Association (ALA) must be brought into the picture at this early stage. Over the years the Association sought to improve library service of all types and it had a definite impact at various strategic points, particularly on public libraries.

ALA was started back in 1876 in Philadelphia. It was a time of energy and hope for the country as a whole. Three men are given credit as the moving spirits in the formation of the association: scholarly Justin Winsor (Boston Public Library), energetic William F. Poole (Chicago Public Library), and systematic Charles Ammi Cutter (Boston Athenaeum). Melvil Dewey was twenty-five at the time; he served as Secretary of the Conference, he introduced his decimal classification, he advocated simplified spelling, he pushed the metric system—and he rubbed some of the patriarchs wrong with his brash manner.

There were 109 attendees at the Philadelphia conference, 96 men and 13 women. The proportions of women to men has of course been reversed since that time; six of the last ten presidents of the American Library Association have been women. Twenty-four of the original group were public librarians, but "even though the public libraries were in the minority, it was they who controlled the convention."[26] Particular attention was paid to procedures of classification and cataloging—what was termed "bibliothecal science."

The great accomplishment of the 1876 convention was the forming of the American Library Association. Now the aspiring professionals had a center around which they could rally. Promotion of professionalism may be said to be the underlying motivation of ALA from that time to this.

The association pushed on several fronts. Andrew Carnegie turned to it for advice, although he operated for the most part independently. The emerging state library agencies sought guidance from the association, for gathered in it were the leading librarians of the day. In 1903 the organization established a standing committee on library training, to be followed in 1924 by the Board of Education for Librarianship. The latter group went on to accredit library schools and their programs, thus providing the standard that would mark the library profession. There was some criticism of the group when it later accepted the second bachelor's degree for completion of a year of graduate education (later moved up to the master's level). Over the years, the Board and its accreditation program provided the framework within which the schools developed.

A consistent aim and role of ALA has been in improving the quality of library service. The first standards for public libraries were promulgated by the Association in 1933, and then a more extensive and formal statement in 1943.[27] A national plan for the public library service appeared under the auspices of the association in 1948.[28] ALA was one of the proponents of the outside sociological appraisal of the institution in 1950, the Public Library inquiry.[29] Later it took the lead when the focus shifted from the outside uniform standards that all libraries were expected to achieve to local planning by each agency to create goals and objectives suited to its individual aims, needs, and resources.[30] Each of these landmark reports will be fitted into the story as this history proceeds.

The association is not an abstract structure that produced standards out of some secret treasure trove that it possessed. ALA is its members and its headquarters staff. The various projects were conceived and carried out by its members. The association identified needs, mobilized committees and groups, provided funds if needed, and published the results in the end. The standards that appeared from time to time came out of the insight, research, and opinions of individual members. The association attracted the movers and shakers who wanted change and improvement and then sought out librarians and other specialists who analyzed problems and proposed solutions.

The national group early on took a firm and consistent stand on intellectual freedom in library collections, adopting a Freedom to Read statement that in turn was adopted as policy by public library boards. It launched a program of publication which spread the principles and expertise of the growing profession.

Along with improvement of library service, ALA has been preoccupied with librarians—their image, their welfare, and their concerns. Those officers concerned with policy and program have had to watch to keep a balance between who librarians are on the one hand and what they do on the other, and their status in the society and their contribution to the society. At various stages the balance has tipped one way or the other. Nor are the needs and aspirations of library personnel all the same; think of the differences between a librarian on the bookmobile in Iowa and the subject specialist in a great research library, and all between the two. This is not a uniform profession, with all practitioners sitting neatly in offices.

ALA established an office for national lobbying in Washington, which led to federal financial aid to libraries in the 1950s and 1960s. Wherever one touches the library movement of the twentieth century, the American Library Association is likely to be present either in a leadership or a supporting role.

All this was not accomplished without internal friction and tension along the way. Some groups felt that they were pushed into back seats in the organization. Some groups of librarians have simply gone their own way and set up separate associations, as in the case of special librarians. There is a separate Catholic Library Association and an American Association of Law Librarians, and several others. ALA itself has come to have a most extensive organization, with divisions, boards, round tables and anything else that will accommodate different interests and positions. Public librarians themselves have an "association" within the overall structure. One respected critic engaged in a dialogue with the then director of ALA, stressing the bureaucracy of the organization and the restlessness of various subgroups.[31] Nor has the association been free of the personal infighting that besets any large group of ambitious individuals. This factionalism continues to the end of the century when it actually becomes hard to hold on to individuals in the leading position of executive director of the association.

Yet ALA, now over fifty-five thousand strong, holds together and exerts a steady influence. Two fundamental purposes persuade and unify the organization. It is the overall assembly and rallying point for librarians, their professional home. And it is the promoter of library service in all its forms, a public relations organization in the best sense.

Recently, the American Library Association has adopted its Goals 2000 to guide the organization and the institution into the next century. This history will analyze the importance of the statement when it speculates on the role of the public library in the Information Age. For the present, the reader will note the hand of the association as this history proceeds.

## Gallery of Administrative Leaders

In the first two decades of the century, American public libraries were fortunate to attract administrators with vision and management skill. These leaders proceeded to fashion the emerging institution into shape and to lay a foundation that would serve in the years ahead. What they envisioned is not too different from the public library that we have a hundred years later.

Despite their personal differences, these individuals had three qualities in common. They were leaders—that is, they set forth goals and then rallied staff to follow them. They had a common purpose—to make the library a resource for a wider segment of the population, a peoples' institution. And their underlying purpose, never clearly articulated, was to make the agency a source of enrichment—an essential element in the quality of life in their communities.

Many of them were men, for this was the gender favored by appointing authorities. But there were women among these early leaders and they made their mark. The leaders built up libraries in large cities and also in smaller towns, and even in rural counties.

Only a sample of administrative leaders is included here. The roster of persons who took hold and built would consume many pages in this book.

### John Shaw Billings (1838–1913)

Billings brought together the Astor, Lenox and Tilden collections to form the New York Public Library. This was in 1896, after he had organized the U.S. Surgeon-General's Library, which became the National Library of Medicine. His early training was in medicine. In New York he supervised everything from a cataloging system to the design of the landmark New York Public Library building in 1911. He set up two distinct divisions, the Research Library and the Circulating Library for branch service. His conception for the Research Library was that of a scholar's library, equal to or greater than the largest university collections. In his regime, the staff grew from forty-two to over one thousand individuals. A commanding and forceful individual, Billings was very versatile, however, with interest in the whole range of library services.

### Arthur E. Bostwick (1860–1942)

Bostwick built up the St. Louis Public Library in his period as director from 1909 to 1938. The institution opened a new building in 1912, moved from four to nineteen branches and tripled its circulation. Bostwick was one of the early missionary leaders in the public library field, with a deep belief in what he termed popular education. He had been trained in physics, in which he earned a Ph.D. degree, and he kind of backed into library work.

Yet he compiled the first systematic treatment of the emerging institution in his *American Public Library* (1910). He was active in the American Library Association, serving as its president in 1907–8. And he was a leader in community groups in St. Louis.

### William Howard Brett (1846–1918)

In his thirty-four years as director of the Cleveland Public Library, Brett brought the institution to the forefront of city libraries. With no college degree or professional education, he moved from a position as salesman in a bookstore to his life work in the library. Brett is given credit for a long list of innovations in service: open shelves, children's service, subject departmentation, a guide to periodical articles. He was animated by a concept of access to books, and with his enthusiasm, he influenced a variety of young people to enter the library profession. He helped to transform the role of the public library. Brett, a man of limited formal education, actually started a library school at Case Western Reserve University and became its first dean.

### Gratia Countryman (1866–1953)

Countryman started as an assistant in the Minneapolis Public Library in 1889 in her twenties, and became head of the agency in 1904 at age thirty-eight. A small woman with a warm smile, she also was forward-looking and decisive. She joined the missionary fold: she built a library that reached out to people. She extended the organization to Hennepin County. Again we have a leader who found her professional base in the American Library Association, of which she was president from 1933–34. She held on to 1936 at age 70, and left another of the public libraries sustained by the progressive growth of the country in the early years of the century.

### John Cotton Dana (1856–1929)

This is perhaps the most independent and restless man in our small gallery. He trained as a lawyer and worked as a surveyor before moving into the library field at age thirty-three. He built up the libraries in Denver (1889–1897), Springfield, Massachusettes (1898–1901), and Newark, New Jersey (1902 until his death). He was skillful at publicity for the library, he established children's rooms, and he built up the business, medical, and foreign-language collections. During his tenure, the Newark library grew in collection from 79,000 to 400,000 volumes, in registrants from 20,000 to 90,000 and in circulation from 300,000 to 1,800,000. Dana was active in the American Library Association, yet he was a consistent critic of the organization, and was a founder of the Special Libraries Association. His special interest was art, and he organized the Newark Art Museum.

**Linda Eastman (1867–1963)**

Eastman served as vice librarian of the Cleveland Public Library for twenty-two years under William Howard Brett, and then twenty years (1918–38) as head of the agency. She carried on the Brett initiatives and added many of her own: business information service, a travel section, service to hospitals and to the blind. Like Brett, she had the quality of inspiring staff to provide thorough service and to try new methods. This is another of the presidents of the American Library Association, in 1928–29. Eastman carried the Cleveland Library through the depression, despite reductions in funds which forced the closing of branches. Like the other early leaders, she was motivated by the concept of the public library as a source of enrichment for people.

**Samuel Swett Green (1837–1918)**

Like some others of the leaders, Green tried other careers before settling on librarianship; he went to divinity school and entered banking. At age thirty-three he was appointed head of the modest library in Worcester, Massachusetts. He expanded the agency in several directions: he reached out to factory workers, he provided service to schools, opened on Sundays, and held art exhibits. His distinctive contribution was in increasing reference service which was just coming into place at the beginning of the century. Green is not considered part of the front rank of early library administrators, but he built a significant service program in a modest-sized city, and he wrote widely about his efforts in the professional literature, thus influencing many librarians seeking to find their way in similar circumstances.

**Harry Miller Lydenberg (1874–1960)**

Lydenberg came into the New York Public Library (NYPL) as an assistant cataloger. A small, quiet, spare man, he became assistant to Billings in 1899, and he supervised the move into the new building in 1911. Moving slowly but steadily upward he became assistant director in 1934 and director in 1941, at age sixty-seven. His first love was research material; he was never happier than when he was sent to Europe to buy rare books. He acquired the Berg Collection of English and American Literature and the Stokes collection of historical prints. At the same time he encouraged development of the branch division and the pioneering work at NYPL in children's service, young people's service, and renders advisory work. On retirement he organized the Biblioteca Benjamin Franklin in Mexico City and the International Relations Office of the American Library Association. Those of us who were entering the field in the early decades remember him as a moderate and supportive presence and as a person of sure, balanced judgment.

**Minerva Sanders (1837–1912)**

Sanders demonstrated that the evolving concept of public-library service could be carried out in a small library. She was head of the Pawtucket, Rhode Island Public Library for thirty-five years, until 1910. She adopted open shelves from the beginning, built collections of both reference and local history, visited schools, delivered to textile mills, and circulated pictures. Her particular interest was in service to children: she broke the custom of excluding young people under twelve or fourteen years of age and worked with children both individually and in groups. In an agency of this size the single "librarian" could give individual service, personal and continuous, over time. With wide literary background and personal commitment, Saunders promoted the "companionship of books."

**Katherine L. Sharp (1865–1914)**

There also were early leaders in education for librarianship, of which Katherine Sharp is a notable example. She started the library school at Armour Institute in Chicago, which then moved to the University of Illinois, and which she directed from 1893 to 1907. She herself was a product of the New York State Library School in Albany. She raised the entrance requirement at Illinois from two years to three years and then to college graduation. This was consistent with her view that librianship was the organization of printed materials for use and required a broad background. She had to recruit faculty and organize the texts for instruction, and she introduced apprenticeship into the curriculum, a provision that later fell by the wayside. She ran a sociable school, with easy relations between students and faculty. Sharp retired to the Lake Placid Club which Melvil Dewey had established in upstate New York.

### Mary L. Titcomb (1857–1931)

When Titcomb organized the Washington County Library in Maryland in 1901, the county was an agricultural area with a scattered population, no high school and no bookstore. Here was a very different setting from the big cities. Within a few years she had no less than sixty-six deposit stations spread over the county, in post offices, general stores, and Sunday schools. She started the Book Wagon in 1904, the vehicle pulled by mules which then moved to a motorized vehicle in 1916. All of these were "firsts"—the county base of organization, the heavy use of deposit stations, and the Book Wagon. Titcomb even added a training class for library recruits. Described as having initiative, energy, and foresight, she brought reading and education to an area in which books had little place in the lives of people. In the total sweep of the public-library movement, Washington County was a small sideshow, but it demonstrated that library service was not just for the educated folks in the cities.

## Notes

1. Oscar Handlin, *The Americans*. (Boston: Little, Brown, 1963), 317.
2. U.S. Bureau of Education. *Statistics of Libraries and Library Legislation in the United States, 1895–1896*. (Washington, D.C.: Government Printing Office, 1897).

3. Louise Barnett, "A History of the Akron Public Library, 1874–1942." (master's thesis, Kent State University, 1974).

4. Sidney Ditzion, *Arsenals of a Democratic Culture; A Social History of the American Public Library Movement in New England and the Middle States from 1850–1900.* (Chicago: American Library Association, 1947).

5. Ibid., 51–76.

6. Robert E. Lee, *Continuing Education for Adults Through the American Public Library, 1833–1964.* (Chicago: American Library Association, 1966).

7. Jesse Shera, *Foundations of the Public Library.* (Chicago: University of Chicago Press, 1949).

8. Jesse Shera, *Knowing Books and Men; Knowing Computers Too.* (Littleton, Colo: Libraries Unlimited, 1973), 184.

9. Ibid., 184.

10. Dee Garrison, *Apostles of Culture: The Public Librarian and American Society, 1876–1920.* (New York: Free Press, 1970), XIII

11. Ibid., xiii.

12. Michael H. Harris, "Purpose of the American Public Library; a Revisionist Interpretation of History." *Library Journal.* vol. 98 (1973), 2509–14.

13. Phyllis Dain, "Ambivalence and Paradox." *Library Journal.* vol. 100 (1975), 261–266.

14. Dee Garrison, *Apostles of Culture,* 222–23

15. Andrew Carnegie, *The Gospel of Wealth.* (Cambridge, Mass.: Harvard University Press, 1962), 50.

16. Ibid., 14.

17. Joseph Wall, *Andrew Carnegie.* (New York: Oxford University Press, 1970).

18. Michael H. Harris, *History of Libraries in the Western World.* 4th ed. (Metuchen, N.J.: Scarecrow Press, 1995), 246–47.

19. George S. Bobinski. *Carnegie Libraries; their History and Impact on American Library Development.* (Chicago: American Library Association, 1969), 20.

20. Abigail A. Van Slyck, *Free to All: Carnegie Libraries and American Culture, 1890–1920.* (Chicago: University of Chicago Press, 1996).

21. George S. Bobinski, *Carnegie Libraries,* 201

22. George S. Bobinski, "Carnegies: Many Have Been Ruined, Remodeled or Both: A New Report on the Status of a Legacy." *American Libraries,* vol. 21 (1990), 296–98.

23. Alex Ladenson, *American Library Laws.* (Chicago: American Library Association, 1983), 1302.

24. Arthur E. Bostwick, *The American Public Library.* (New York: Appleton, 1929), 9.

25. E. S. Wilkes, "Open Shelves for Large Libraries." *Library Journal,* vol. 25 (1900), 113

26. Edward Holley, "Raking the Historical Coals: The American Library Association Beginnings," in *Reader in American Library History,* ed. Michael M. Harris (Washington, D.C.: Microcard Editions, 1971), 183.

27. *Post-War Standards for Public Libraries.* (Chicago: American Library Service. Chicago, American Library Association, 1948).

28. Carleton B. Joeckel, *A National Plan for Public Library Service* (Chicago: American Library Association), 1948.

29. Robert D. Leigh, *The Public Library in the United States.* (New York: Columbia University Press, 1950).

30. Vernon E. Palmour, *A Planning Process for Public Libraries.* (Chicago: American Library Association, 1980).

31. Ralph E. Ellsworth, "Critique of Library Associations in America." *Library Quarterly,* vol. 21 (1961), 382–400.

# 3

# The Innovative Years, 1918–1929

The first symbol that comes to mind for the 1920s is the Charleston, perhaps the most ungainly dance ever devised. Women bobbed their hair and shortened their skirts, and men and women filled the speakeasies. Jazz was the rage, with its unconventional rhythm and its musical improvisation on the horns, the saxophone, and the clarinet. Or should the symbol be bathtub gin, for these were the wonderfully wacky years of Prohibition.

But behind the glitter, substantial gains were made, on the social front, on the industrial front, and on the library front. Millions of families worked their way into the middle class; their children would grow up to become the professional and business people of the 1950s and after. Out of this same background came the library leaders who would direct the institution in the latter half of the century.

Cities grew apace. They were laid out on a checkerboard pattern—easy to get around, easy to locate the center—that was efficient but monotonous and dull. Americans are surprised and charmed by the more natural and organic character of European cities. A person dropped into the center of Paris or Rome or Athens would promptly recognize the place, but anyone dropped into the middle of Kansas City or Dallas or Atlanta could only guess.

The city rapidly became the focus of marketing, finance, information, and cultural life. Families moving into the middle class would have a house (with a mortgage) on a side street, and young couples and individuals would have an apartment somewhere near the center. Parents and children alike would absorb the culture (some from the public library) and thus become full-fledged Americans.

There were 15 million automobiles on the road by 1923, and twice that number at the end of the decade. The Federal Aid Road Act of 1920 vastly increased the number of roads in the country. As a result new shopping patterns appeared, central "consumer's palaces" (Marshall Field's in Chicago, Macy's in New York, and Wanamaker's in Philadelphia) and chain stores (Atlantic and Pacific, Walgreen, and Woolworth's): even Christmas became a "festival of consumption."[1]

The system worked to promote standardization and conformity. Fashion prevailed in clothing. Almost every household turned on the radio every night and listened to the same programs (Rudy Vallee or Amos and Andy). Movies showing sophisticated upper-class life were popular or you could see a fairy tale with Mary Pickford or Rudolph Valentino; 40 million movie seats sold every week. If a person wanted to escape from the standardized culture, where did you turn—except to the public library?

Books and magazines also carried the same message, whether Emily Post's *Etiquette* of 1923 or Anita Loos' *Gentlemen Prefer Blondes* of 1926. No less than ten magazines circulated 2.5 million copies per issue (*Reader's Digest*, *Time*, etc.) and dozens others passed the 1 million mark. Both the Book-of-the-Month Club and the Literary Guild were launched in this period. A large readership of popular material came into existence and would affect policies of the public library.

Again there were authors who penetrated below the surface and held the culture up to criticism: Sinclair Lewis in *Main Street* (1920), Edith Wharton in *Age of Innocence* (1920), F. Scott Fitzgerald in *The Great Gatsby* (1925). Some people were shocked by the naturalistic literature. Theodore Dreiser's *Sister Carrie* was suppressed, as was James Joyce's *Ulysses* and James Branch Cabell's *Jurgen*. For this and other periods, read the titles that challenge the approved order and you would be consuming the more substantial items that would endure for some years, while the most popular publications would fade from memory in a short time.

Distinctly American works were also created in the visual arts. The list of painters recognized by this time is impressive: Winslow Homer, Thomas Eakins, George Bellows, James McNeill Whistler, John Singer Sergeant, John Sloan, and Mary Cassatt. Frank Lloyd Wright designed original American structures beginning in the 1920s.

Universal woman's suffrage was finally achieved in 1920 in the United States with passage of the Nineteenth Amendment. By the 1920s coeducation prevailed from the elementary to the college level, the latter in part to prepare women for careers in teaching and in librarianship. But full equality was still to be gained in job opportunities, hiring practices, and salaries—and in the image of women on the part of both sexes.

Other developments marked this colorful decade: Charles Lindbergh flew across the Atlantic, Clarence Darrow and William Cullen Bryant debated evolution, H. L. Mencken mounted his vitriolic campaign against the bourgeois majority. The Ku Klux Klan spread its terror. And sports heroes emerged who are remembered to this day: Babe Ruth, Jack Dempsey, Bobby Jones, and Red Grange.

Compared with Theodore Roosevelt and Woodrow Wilson in the decade before, and with Franklin Roosevelt in the depression years, the presidential leadership of the 1920s was bland and lackluster: Warren Harding, Calvin Coolidge and Herbert Hoover. Coolidge gave us all some homespun advice: "Four-fifths of our troubles in this life would disappear if we would only sit down and keep still."[2] Within cities, party bosses gained control of local politics: Bill Thompson in Chicago, Tom Pendergast in Kansas City, and Boss Tweed in New York. These local bosses were not against public libraries. On the contrary they saw the agency as a source for the plain people that they controlled, a source of information and education for lower- and middle-class families.

America built a wall around itself. It had had enough of war in 1917–1918. The country had recovered from the immediate postwar business slump. Tariffs were increased and foreign entanglements avoided. The country would isolate itself, mind its own business, produce and buy and invest, and have some fun at the same time.

These also were prosperous times, perhaps overly prosperous.

Consumption ruled the land, reinforced by advertising and installment buying. Families emptied their bank accounts not solely for automobiles and kitchen appliances but also to buy land in Florida and to invest in the stock market, often on margin accounts. The stock market went up and up, to the point where individual stocks were grossly overpriced. Then, after a few warning signs, the market crashed on October 24, 1929. Millions of shares were sold as investors large and small ran for cover. Within a few days stocks were down by one-half. By 1930 banks began to fail. Families lost their savings; individuals jumped out of hotel windows.

The Jazz Age ended not with a bang but with a thump.

## Overview of Library Development, 1918–1929

The public library took strength from the vitality of the 1920s. In some respects this would be the most innovative decade of the century for the institution. The focus shifted from collections to readers, from preservation to use. Inventive and dedicated librarians came forward to build a structure of service. This aroused an increase in public esteem and an increase in financial support, which in turn would carry the public library through the coming depression.

This shift of focus from book to reader brought the agency into the lives of people; from being a collection at a distance, catering to bookish individuals, it became a source of stimulation and guidance for a wider segment. A visit to the library was not a trip to a dull enclave with solemn rows of books. There were the children listening open-mouthed to a story or poring through the pictures in a book, there were the mothers at the shelves on household duties or conferring with a librarian on what to read next. There were the business people sitting at tables and going through material on sales and investments, and the teenagers giggling over the romance of a sheik from Arabia, and the elders catching up on a book they had meant to read for some time. Visitors realized that they had come upon some kind of intellectual crossroads, a stimulating marketplace of information, ideas, and expression.

It would be too much to call this the Golden Age of the Public

Library, for the collections in depth and professional staffs were not yet there, but for those of us who started to work in the library at this stage it was a period of promise and inspiration. Workers could palpably feel the impact of their efforts. Those who would lead the public library in the period of expansion after World War II were nourished in the twenties and the thirties.

The groundwork was laid in the 1920s for a range of services that would come to characterize the public library and energize it throughout the twentieth century. The information function—what librarians called "reference"—took firm hold and may preserve the institution over into the twenty-first century, although the agency never did become a primary source of information for a wide segment of the American public. Special collections and programs for children were eagerly received by both the youngsters and their parents and accounted in part for the financial support that libraries received through the years. A similar effort for "young adults"—actually teenagers— started in the 1920s had a more checkered career, essentially because these are complex years and librarians were never able to relate to more than a small portion of the group. The public library, besides supplying books, became a source of stimulation and guidance of reading, partly by featuring selected titles, partly by instituting book reviews and book discussions, and partly by an educational program of reader's advisers. This last specialized service, being a one-on-one activity, proved to be expensive and eventually was pulled back into the reference function. For a period, public libraries were involved in providing collections within schools but in time the schools installed their own libraries. Perhaps the most impressive development of this decade was the emergence of the appearance of skilled and dedicated professionals—innovators and practitioners—within the library staff.

## Adult Reference Service

By the 1920s the public library had a governmental structure, open access, organization of the collection, and an emerging image. An increasingly literate and educated population turned to it for background, for practical help, and for diversion. The home circulation of books from many established libraries doubled in this period.

But readers needed assistance in making full use of this resource. The librarian as guide and interpreter came into the picture. This was a significant step, not so much because of the physical fact of the reference desk, but because of the fresh, more active attitude toward service that it revealed. Earlier there had been only the delivery desk where one asked an attendant for the book desired. Now within the service location there was a staff member standing ready to give help and advise. William Foster, director of the Providence, Rhode Island Public Library is given credit for being one of the first to establish an information desk in a public library,[3] after which Samuel Swett Green proceeded to develop this work in the Worcester, Massachusetts Library. By the 1920s such service points had become a fairly regular feature of larger and medium-sized libraries. A research study in the 1930s found that a service population in the range of fifty thousand was necessary before a library generated enough income to maintain a separate, fully staffed information desk.[4]

At first, librarians used their own term "reference" to identify these locations. The users might be confused by the term, wondering if they needed some kind of reference or recommendation in order to use the library. Over the years the desk more and more became identified simply by the straightforward label of "information."

There are levels of reference work. First is the pure location question: where is the unabridged dictionary, where are the magazines kept? Then there are questions about using the bibliographic facilities: where will I find this book, how do you locate a magazine article? Most common are the straightforward information quests: what is the atomic weight of silver, where is Katmandu? Call this spot information or hit-and-run data. At a more advanced level the inquiry may lead to a literature search, although most public libraries do not often engage in reference service at this depth.

The reference librarian is a kind of traffic officer, directing users into both the physical facilities and the bibliographical facilities. Most libraries try to handle inquiries at one location with one staff group—as though the doctors' office had only one service desk from receptionist to medical specialist given at this point. Later, in larger libraries, there was a division and specialization of the work at the reference station, with subject-specialist librarians in subject rooms. The reader first comes upon the information station where one can get a "quick fix," and then has recourse to the specialists. This later development will be examined in the section about the 1930–45 period.

At the information desk, the reference librarian sometimes provided the requested data directly or sometimes provided the source for users to examine themselves. At times libraries would pull together the facts about an issue—an upcoming election, a public figure, a catastrophe—and reproduce the material for the convenience of curious citizens, the library as small-scale publisher. Reference service was reaching out, becoming more active, connecting with the flow of life. Then there was the telephone, which was in wide use by the 1920s. Some inquirers learned to turn to it to get needed information. A few larger libraries responded by setting up telephone reference lines connected to specially designed data centers. Searchers could get what they wanted without going to the library. This pattern, without an actual visit, would be extended in the next century when the content of the library collection was machine-readable and could be consulted on the home or office computer screen.

In succeeding decades, library reference service became even more reactive, waiting on the inquirer to put the question. Extracting and disseminating data (that is, publishing) became uncommon, primarily because it put a load on limited budgets. The attitude of anticipate-and-disseminate of the earlier years has become more wait-and-respond.

In substance the reference desk added a new function to the public library. The library had been the source of a subject collection and the source of recreational reading. Now it was an information station, there to help searchers to extract data from the record of knowledge. Actually the library never became a primary source of information in the community—the Public Library Inquiry at midcentury was to find that "Only a tiny minority in a national sample of the adult population . . . indicated that they would turn to the public library as a source of information on such subjects as nutrition, child care, or foreign countries." But the function held on, and by the end of the century libraries were trying to see what role this function could play in the Digital Age.

Information service has not only been retained but has become specialized over the years, first with the development of subject divisions (see the 1930–45 period) and more recently with the computerized storage of data (see the 1980–99 period). Public libraries may become the service stations on the Information Highway, for a majority of the population.

## Reader's Advisory Service

A related function had to do with advice on what to read. It was one thing to ask for the population of Ireland or to seek help using the card catalog, but was another to ask what to read for understanding the Scandinavian countries or to appreciate Impressionist art or the discovery of electricity. Early on such inquiries were handled at the reference desk, but they required more thorough book knowledge and also called for a more continuous contact with users. For a period, from the 1920s until World War II, the reader's adviser station came into the picture.

This can properly be called an educational service, over and above the supply function. If education is taken to mean planned action toward articulated goals, then library users provided the goals and library staff provided the planned action. In fact, at times, the staff also provided the goals, in lectures on specific topics, in reading lists devoted to current events, in book displays designed to stimulate the potential interests of patrons. These latter promotional activities helped searchers to identify and define their objectives. A reader might come into the library simply looking for a substantial book for bedtime reading and go out enrolled in a program to understand modern psychology or the Islamic religion.

The reader's adviser was usually located in a quiet corner or a separate office, in contrast with the location of the reference desk which was purposely in the line of traffic. The reader would come in with a topic or interest and wanted advice on what to read. Sometimes a single book recommended by the librarian would serve the purpose. Sometimes a course of reading was necessary, as in examining a historical period or a literary trend or a scientific development. The reader's adviser first attempted to evaluate the seeker's seriousness of purpose, educational background, reading ability, and the like. A sequence of reading would then be set up, with the patron coming in at set intervals to get the next assignment in the sequence. It was surprising and inspiring to see what varied interests readers would come up with and also encouraging to see how some pursued the program to the end—self-education at its best.

The idea caught on and some innovative librarians were drawn to it—for example, Marion Hawes in the Enoch Pratt Free Library of Baltimore and Jennie Flexner in the New York Public Library. Standard reading programs were produced on current topics. The American Library Association issued its "Reading with a Purpose" series, recommendations which libraries purchased and made available. The public library had added an explicit educational objective to its other functions.

But as time went by the reader's advisory service slowly declined, as did parts of the wider adult education movement that had flourished at the turn of the century. The readers inclination to follow a rigorous program was less evident, and libraries found this service expensive and demanding of staff time. Few reader's advisory desks were maintained by libraries at the end of the century. What reading guidance service remains has been absorbed into the reference desk. The questions are likely to be "where" or "what," not "can you recommend." The librarian is more a source of information and less a guide as to what to read.

Therefore, the explicit adult education service, after a promising start, tended to fade into the provision and information functions. Many years later in 1963, one of the proponents of adult education services in the public library, Margaret Monroe, looked back and discerned three successive stages for this activity: early appearance at the fringes of reference service, then a distinct program with its own location and staff, and eventually its absorption widely in the library, in book selection, in reference, and in community work.[5] In her view, the third stage infused other parts, enriching the total program. Another interpretation is that, as explicitly educational service declined, the concept lost force, and the institution shucked off this responsibility and fell back on its supply or provision function, delivering documents. Professor Monroe's analysis came in the 1960s, before adult education had been almost completely absorbed into other basic services. Also, her interpretation was based on tracing developments in three libraries that were not necessarily typical of the wider trend: the Enoch Pratt Library in Baltimore, the New York Public Library, and Kern County, California.

Despite the contraction of reader's advisory services as budgets became tight, the public library still has an educational dimension. People resolve to study a subject and go to the agency to get the necessary material. Where else would they go? It is a source not only for reading material but also for guidance in the world of communications.

## Young Adult Service

Separate staff and facilities for young adults appeared in the 1920s, at least in the larger libraries. This effort was aimed at adolescents or teenagers, with the focus on the thirteen-to-sixteen year range. In essence it was a combination of reader's advisory service and reference service for this strategic age group.

A minority of teenagers went on to high school in the 1920s, so the public library was one of the few educational influences to which many members of this group were exposed. At this level, young people were no longer satisfied with children's literature, nor with such practices as storytelling and puppet shows. At the same time, it was self-evident that these were crucial years in the growth of individuals, years in which special problems and tensions might appear and years in which lifelong attitudes and goals were beginning to be formed. An added incentive for establishing separate young adult service was that high-school students were turning to the newly established reference services of the library, sometimes overcrowding the reference desk; the young adult unit would take some of the strain off other parts of the agency.

Young adult librarians with a special interest in teenagers and with a commitment to help and guide young people in these critical years were hired. A section or separate room was set up for young adult service and publications appealing to this age level were assembled. The young adult librarian was stationed in this room after school hours and at other times when the young people would be able to visit. The staff member also worked outside the building with schools and community groups.

The books assembled were often about teenage characters who were dealing with the problems and adventures of this age group. Family relations, peer relations, and relations with the other sex were stressed. How far to go with explicitly sexual material was a delicate point. The need for guidance was there, but the young people themselves came with different preconceptions and uncertainties about sex. Their parents' beliefs were also a concern, so the topic was often played down or avoided. No doubt some young adult librarians took an additional step and sought to protect young readers from questionable publications, but its difficult to hold off the real world from young people.

Individual work with teenagers often brought librarians face to face with the emotional and value problems of this age level: career goals, self-confidence, divorce, and the lure of drugs (later in the century). Staff members had no easy or ready answers. They could only turn to resources on the shelves and hopefully could hit the mark by wise selection. This was the librarian as counselor. It must be admitted that most staff members proceeded with limited training in psychology and in adolescence in particular. Empathy was their main resource.

What was the young adult librarian seeking to achieve? What was the goal of the service? There was no one answer, and no doubt different staff members emphasized different goals, but a predominant objective was to make lifelong readers of their clientele and at the same time to help them on the road to maturity. In this sense it was a form of the reader's advisory service but with an added element of effecting change and development in individuals.

Two goals predominated among these librarians. One was to nurture the love of reading as a source of enjoyment, stimulation, and aesthetic experience, similar to the basic goal of the children's service. The other more practical and utilitarian goal was to develop the habit of turning to printed sources for guidance in making personal decisions. The school had taught the skill of reading; the library would show what the skill was for. The second goal was the more uncertain because it moved into unchartered waters which had the librarian guiding the value systems and life ambitions of teenagers.

Response to the service from adolescents was never very strong. Some welcomed the selection of material for them and also appreciated the advice from the librarians. In some instances staff members attracted groups that met together, discussed mutual interests, exchanged views on what had been read, and even put on modest dramatic presentations. This staff did not reach out to many parents, nor were they able to work regularly with many individual teenagers over a period of years; the young clientele tended to drift away from the agency, often after graduating from high school. It should be noted that youth librarians did influence publishers to issue books for this age group.

Several factors worked against the young adult service. The hard reality is that many teenagers were not particularly in search of outside guidance and might even be suspicious of adults who they saw as prying into their lives. On the other side of the equation, we have referred to limitations on the part of some young adult librarians in working with adolescents. Further, just as this service got underway, attendance at high schools increased, and some schools had their own libraries. Another stumbling block was that almost all young adult librarians in the service were women; only a small minority of users were young men who were willing to turn to older women for guidance.

The advocates of service to young adults make a positive case for its significance and accomplishments. Miriam Braverman traces the origin and growth of the service in 1920 and the following years in three centers; the New York Public Library (Mabel Williams and Margaret Scoggin were the moving spirits), the Cleveland Public Library (Jean Roos), and the Enoch Pratt Free Library in Baltimore (Margaret Edwards).[6] She notes how early librarians had to overcome their hostility toward young people. She pays tribute to the programs developed: "They were shaped first by the personalities and talents of the coordinators, all of whom were women of strong conviction."[7] And she recognizes the decline of young adult services by the 1950s. By 1975 full-time staff members for the young adult service were uncommon.

It would be overly critical to call this a marginal service because for a period in the 1920s and 1930s it had a notable vigor and intensity, some of which hangs on to the present day. Late in the century a cadre of young adult librarians still pushed their cause and issued a listing of outstanding programs still in existence.[8] Some of the large central buildings constructed recently have set aside distinct areas for young adults. This is a garden that flourished and then faded, but still holds on where dedicated gardeners cultivate it.

## Children's Service

Unlike the young adult service, no reservations need be expressed about the success and durability of the specialized library service to younger readers, from pre-school up to the teens. This started around the turn of the century, was built up in the 1920s, and continues strong to this day.

Prior to 1900, most of the earliest public libraries actually did not serve children; they restricted access to those over twelve or fourteen. Brookline, Massachusetts, is given credit for the first children's room. But the idea did not spread rapidly, for it was felt that the presence of youngsters would disturb serious adult readers. Slowly the doors were opened to the younger generation in the first decade or two of the century, preparing the way for the leap forward in the 1920s.

Today, in the minds of both the general public and of government officials, it is one of the main reasons for supporting the public library. This supportive view remains even though schools teach reading and schools probably have their own libraries. A sociological appraisal of the institution in 1950 concluded that children's service was its "classic success."[9]

From the beginning children's librarians have stressed quality and substance in the books provided. Cartoon-type material was rejected. Literature for children is imaginative and appealing. Its quality is quite high and has been maintained at this level by the influence of juvenile librarians and by the Newbery and Caldecott awards for children's literature which they sponsor. Librarians prompted the establishment of juvenile departments within major publishing houses in the 1920s. As one of the main purchasers of books, librarians set the criteria for what publishers issued.

Children went along with "Johnny Crow who would dig and sow," joined Madeline when she had to go to the hospital, and marveled at the Wild Things of Maurice Sendak, not excluding Dr. Seuss's Cat in the Hat and the Grinch Who Stole Christmas. These were more than comic-book characters. And children came up with questions that tested librarians to the full: Do you have the recipe for a caveman's meal?

Very soon children's librarians became quite specialized. Special courses for the work were provided in library schools. They knew the literature thoroughly and they got their satisfaction from working with youngsters. They developed the art of storytelling, holding young folks in thrall with tales of animals, adventures, and other children. This was particularly appealing in a time before constant listening and viewing of radio and television. Special credit goes to Augusta Baker of the New York Public Library for encouraging the development and promotion of storytelling.[10]

Other forms of stimulation were used: puppet shows, dramatizations by youngsters, and vacation reading clubs. Class visits were made. Communication was nurtured in all its forms, setting children on a road that served many of them all their lives. One slogan that was used in the earlier years was "the right book for the right child at the right time." More recently the cereal box announced that "Children who read — succeed." The faith was expressed in these terms:

> Tomorrow's solution to a highly technical and economically critical social problem may likely spring from the very same imagination that was stimulated long before by a library storyteller's tale.[11]

The pioneer Augusta Baker described the purpose of children's service simply: "to contribute to lifelong competence and self-fulfillment." These high ideals prevailed among children's librarians through the years, even while adult librarians were arguing education versus recreation, and information versus reading guidance.

In the early decades juvenile librarians worked more with grade-school youngsters. Then when libraries became established in elementary schools, the staff turned more to pre-school programs, for the four year and five year olds and even for toddlers. It is heartwarming to see the young ones, and their mothers, having what is evidently a satisfying and often a noisy time in the local library.

But there were individuals who did not respond; books and reading had very little place in their lives. Causes can be traced back to families. Parents who did not read much beside the newspaper did not motivate youngsters to try the printed page. Nor would such parents be likely to make the effort of taking their children to the library in those years before they could make the trip themselves. Fortunate were the youngsters who stumbled upon the library or were taken there by friends, for a whole new world opened to them, rich, colorful, exciting and useful.

Did all the children who responded go on to become lifelong readers? Of course not. Libraries are not noted for follow-up, for seeking to determine the results of their ministrations. But testimony by adults regularly turns up that attests to a considerable measure of success, for stories are told of memories of early years in the children's room.

The names of early children's librarians include Anne Carroll Moore and Augusta Baker in New York City, Effie Power in Cleveland, and Francis Sayers in Pittsburgh, followed by regiments of specialists to this day. These and others truly deserve the label of "innovators." In larger cities central coordinators of children's work developed programs throughout the branches, such as Agatha Shea in Chicago. Because the work was specialized, children's librarians were not often transferred to other library services, nor were they promoted to general administration, which was a source of dissatisfaction among some in the ranks; very few children's librarians became the directors of large libraries.

In the 1920s and 1930s juvenile registrants often constituted one-third of the users of public libraries, and juvenile literature accounted for one-half of home circulation. An extraordinary service had been launched, and almost a century later it still stands out and engenders the strongest of public approval. There is a formula here for success: (1) a clear purpose, (2) dedicated personnel, and (3) a concentration of effort.

## Promotion of Reading

An important additional step in user-oriented service must be added for this period—the promotion of reading. The services just described—reference and reader's advisory work—were there for people who sought them out. But there were other potential readers who did not turn to the public agency. The next step was to "sell" the nonusers on coming to this people-oriented institution that had grown up nearby. This fresh emphasis could be put under the educational function of the library, for librarians were now identifying goals for the user and also selecting means to achieve the goals, a little like a college advertising its programs of study. Or a different analogy would be to use the term "missionary work" to characterize the promotion of reading. Not just the converted who came seeking service but others who would benefit were now the target.

A merchandising approach was used, similar to that employed by commercial retail enterprises. First the library engaged in publicity, informing the populace of the existence of the agency and what it had to offer—getting the attention of the "customer." This was done in newspapers, on the radio, with flyers, and right down to window displays. Inside the library, eye-catching displays were mounted, almost like "loss leaders" in retailing. There were the shelves or racks of new books. Not too far behind would be a display case of old favorites, with the popular titles of yesteryear. Subject topics were often chosen for the displays, such as biography or travel. More specific interests were identified, whether home repair, child care, gardening, modern art, salesmanship, health or hobbies—the gamut of human attention. More formal disciplines, such as economics, anthropology or philosophy, were usually avoided, for the library was responding to popular adult interests, seeking to connect library use to the daily lives of people.

The seasons often brought on more promotional activity, for Christmas or Easter or summer sports. Upcoming elections or a local civic issue might be featured. Then there were the sections of mysteries and westerns. Walk into a library and stimulation and temptation were all about.

Nor were promotional activities limited to displays and book racks. Reading lists were provided, either compiled by the local library or obtained from the American Library Association, which still maintained its "Reading with a Purpose" series. Lists and recommendations were put into local newspapers. Some librarians achieved considerable visibility by compiling and publishing lists of "The Best Books of the Year," even before the *New York Times* and other newspapers compiled such lists.

And staff went out—to women's clubs, to church groups, to Rotary Club and Kiwanis meetings, and to union groups. The librarian was the book person, the book expert, and was respected as such. If they knew so much about publications, why not go into the library and ask for material about one's personal interests? Later in the century a few libraries even had television studios in which programs were prepared to get the library message on the air.

A dramatic example of the effect of promotion was the increase in circulation in the Enoch Pratt Library of Baltimore in the 1920s. When Joseph L. Wheeler came into the directorship of the library and instituted his policy of promotion of reading, book circulation increased from 1,004,061 in 1925 to 2,491,174 in 1929, more than doubling in five years.[12] No one cause accounted for the increase, for the library also opened up its closed stacks and changed its book selection policies. A multipronged effort was aimed at promotion of reading.

While tracing the promotion of reading by libraries in the remaining years of the century, we will see some falling off as budgets became tight and other demands increased. Field visits to groups outside the library were the first to go. Reading lists became less frequent. Displays within libraries were reduced in number, and mostly with general themes rather than current interests. Public libraries in the 1990s are closer to the wait-and-serve institutions of the first years and less like the outreach agencies of the 1920s and after. Has some of the missionary spirit been lost?

## Service to Schools

At the same time that the public library was expanding its services to the general public, the question arose of providing materials to students in schools. Of course schools had books, in the form of textbooks and possibly a bookcase in a corner of the classroom. Students could turn to the public library for supplementary materials, and the more motivated did so. But the effort to enrich teaching and to open the world of knowledge to young people led to interest in developing collections within school buildings.

It was natural to turn to the existing public library for the materials needed in formal education, at least in the larger cities with their more established general agencies. Staff in the public library knew books and their organization into collections. Further, it seemed more efficient and more economical to have a single agency serving young people in and out of school, rather than having one collection on the main street and another in the school building.

Public libraries responded in different ways to the school's demand. The most frequent provision was in the form of classroom collections loaned for a period from the central city collections. Titles could be selected that were particularly needed in the individual room, depending on subject matter and level of instruction. The deposit collections could be shifted and replaced as the topics of study changed. Once started, the demand for this service increased to the point where it was a rare classroom in some cities that did not have some reading materials from the public library.

But the very success of this approach led to its demise. Because the demand was so great, the question of expense and finance came to the fore. The cost of maintaining a school's deposit department and of providing thousands of books came at a time when the public library was trying to build services to the general public. And just ahead were the very lean years of the depression.

Even more basic was the surge in demand from teachers and students. Once they had the asset of a collection of books close at hand, they wanted more. Formal education was changing in this period, becoming more varied and enriched, seeking to reach all of the students—the result of the challenge of John Dewey and others, and the result of more vital training of teachers in schools of education. Libraries became an essential resource in schools.

An effort to meet this need took the form of actual school libraries staffed and administered by the public library. This was the arrangement for a period, for example, in Chicago. The staff members operating the school libraries were actually on the payroll of the public library and were supervised by a central schools department maintained by the same agency. Within the schools there was also inevitable supervision by the school principal, a divided structure that could not endure. The librarian tried to function as an integral part of the teaching staff, but was usually seen as an outsider. The librarian lacked the training and skill to instruct students in the use of the library and to work with teachers in instructional projects. The school needed its own library and its own librarian.

Another short-lived version was the school-housed branch library. The idea here was to serve both the general public and students within the school with one installation. During the school day the library would serve the pupils and teachers and then remain open in the evenings and Saturdays to serve the community. Some administrators defended this plan but in most instances it was judged not to serve either purpose very well. For one thing, adults did not take favorably to the requirement of going to a school building to get their reading. For another, controversy arose over practical matters like keeping the building open and dividing costs for utilities and physical maintenance.

There were two dynamic forces at work here, the drive of the community for adequate library service and the drive of the school for its own facility as part of the educational process. Inevitably the two agencies had to separate. But it can be said that the public library did help to implant the seed that led to the great movement for school media centers. This movement went forward even during the depression years and by 1944 there were separate standards for school libraries adopted by the American Library Association: *School Libraries for Today and Tomorrow: Functions and Standards.*

The question of providing library service to children and young people through both the school library and the public library remains to this day. On the one hand is the media center in the school building, handy to all students, open every school day. On the other hand are the children's and young adult sections in the public library, open after school, on Saturdays, and during vacations. Both are supported from tax money. What about combining the two in one facility?

Theoretically, the reason for maintaining both is that the school teaches reading whereas the public library provides the means to utilize that skill. But this over-simplifies the relationship. The teacher and the school librarian also instruct young people on using resources and also encourage outside reading. The reason that the two agencies continue is that the children's section in the public library—with its effective service program—has carved out a place for itself which is honored by both officials and parents. In fact some parents would likely come out in favor of the public library if a choice had to be made between either a general facility or a school facility.

I recall with a smile an assignment I received in the 1920s when I was a junior clerk in the public library. I was sent as an attendant to the library in a night school located in a school building. On the first night the principal of the night school bustled in to greet what he called his "new librarian." He promptly asked me to give a talk about the library to the teachers. This was not exactly an assignment for a junior clerk, but I did the best I could. The principal continued to promote the use of the library. Later in the semester, to my complete surprise, he was indicted for misuse of school funds. I gathered from this that one must be careful with principals who are very enthusiastic about the library—they may be dishonest!

Having the public library maintain the school library was not a tenable arrangement. School officials wanted their own libraries and their own librarians. Unfortunately the pendulum in some cases has swung to the other extreme, with nearby school and public libraries having little cooperation and indeed little communication. Joint operation is now an episode of the past.

This is another example of a service started by the public library, which was brought up to a substantial level, and which then fell back or faded. The readers advisory service is another example and to some extent young adult service and business service. The institution seemed to search out the new services, as though it were trying to see where it fit in, and then for one reason or another downgraded or reduced the effort. For all the progress made, the public library still was seeking to clarify its mission.

## Emergence of Professional Personnel

Who were the staff members who originated, built up, and provided the new reader services? What was their general education? Where did they get their technical training? These questions apply not just to the leaders in a few very large cities but to staff in the many centers across the land that were adding reference service, children's activities, and adult-education programs.

The simple answer was not that the innovators and skilled workers came from formal library schools in institutions of higher learning. Although some did follow that route, only a half-dozen schools existed in the 1920s. The Williamson report and the establishment of the school at Columbia University came in the mid-twenties. The originators were already on the job by that time.

It was not a matter of new graduate library schools producing advanced professionals who then went out and established reference, reader's advisory, and children's services. No, for the most part these innovations resulted from recruits from the ranks who reacted to the challenge. In time the graduate schools provided skilled technicians to staff the special services already in existence. In fact the schools grew in number and flourished because the jobs already existed and the demand was there. Education followed innovation, not the other way around.

Special credit must be given to a remarkable group of individuals who did not have extensive formal education and who picked up their library background by experience, trial and error, and occasional classes. They might have some college credits or they might be only high-school graduates. They were among those who had been recruited and hired to carry on the routine business of the library and who proved to have special ability and dedication that marked them out from the group. As one or another reader's service was instituted, they were designated to do the work. Many met the challenge. We have biographical records of the outstanding leaders;[13] it would be interesting to have the record of those other unsung individuals who rose to the occasion.

For library attendants in the ranks who responded and handled the new reader services and also the administration of branches, genuine career opportunities opened up. These were mostly women. In my first years in the field, I worked for several such women, no one of whom was a library school graduate and some of whom were not college graduates.

Some of the larger cities—Chicago, Baltimore, Cleveland, and others—established organized training classes to which the new aspirants turned. The classes were taught by the innovators who had originated the services, or by a "faculty" of one person also recruited from the ranks. Sometimes staff members from other libraries were admitted, making the training classes informal local library schools. Recruits occasionally went off for a period and worked in a service already established, thus getting training on the job. All in all, this was a fragmentary, incomplete program of preparation for an emerging profession.

As noted, the bulk of the staff members providing the new services were women. One account reports that 90 percent of library personnel by 1920 were women.[14] Library service opened up one career opportunity for women at a time when there were few such opportunities. If one did not elect teaching, nursing, or perhaps social work, there was librarianship. This was the positive side.

But there was another side to what has been called the feminization of the profession, with negative results.[15] One was low salaries in library work, for recruits could be readily found from the feminine ranks. Another was the relatively low ceiling on the library career, because the higher administrative positions went mostly to men, this being a time when library boards and appointing officials shared the general prejudice against women executives.

Even the question of whether library service is a profession can be traced back to this early time when women came to predominate in the ranks. It has taken time for women to be recognized and respected as practicing professionals. These characteristics of library careers—relatively low salaries, low career ceilings, and uncertain professional image—still hold.

The 1920s also saw the foundation of formal library education for professional service, which shortly would take over from the local training classes. The signal and beacon for this strategic development was the Williamson report of 1923.[16] Charles Williamson, a social scientist turned librarian, made a convincing case for extensive preparation for library service. He recommended (1) a full undergraduate subject education before taking up professional training, (2) affiliation of graduate library schools with universities, (3) a two-year program of graduate education, and (4) creation of a postprofessional research program leading to a Ph.D. degree. Williamson based his case on the wide subject background needed to evaluate and select publications for collections and to organize this material, and on the reader services being instituted by various types of libraries.

This was a turning point. Columbia University established a professional school along the lines recommended by Williamson, and other institutions followed shortly. Most adopted a one-year rather than a two-year graduate sequence and awarded a second bachelor's degree, the bachelor of library service.

Other schools did not follow the Williamson doctrine but established a professional sequence within the undergraduate years. They were recognized by state accrediting groups and concentrated more on producing school librarians. Some remain to this day, so that there is not one clear avenue for preparing for library service. But it was the graduate programs that predominated and in time gained accreditation from the American Library Association.

Actually, public libraries did not at first make as much use of the new graduate programs as did academic and scholarly libraries. They continued to depend on exceptional individuals in their clerical ranks, and the training classes within libraries continued for a few decades. Slowly a distinct professional class of positions was established, requiring a college degree plus a year of graduate-level library study. This did not occur, for example, in the Chicago Public Library for thirty years, until the 1950s.

A Carnegie grant had financed the Williamson report, and an additional grant from the same source carried out another of Williamson's recommendations, the establishment of an advanced center to provide research underpinnings for library service. This was established at the University of Chicago, (see developments in the 1930s). The 1920s saw the foundation of a genuine profession coming into place. There was an active national association, a growing body of literature, and now graduate professional curricula and a research center. All that will happen later, up to the advent of the computer, will depend upon the educational programs and the professional standards which appeared in the 1920s and years immediately following. From this source will come the leaders and skilled practitioners for the remainder of the century. For all the changes in accreditation standards over the next decades and the adoption of the master's degree, education for library service has not changed that much since then.

## Gallery of Service Innovators

The distinctive services just described provided the framework for public-library development throughout the century. They did not occur by themselves. Individuals envisioned the possibilities, tried out various approaches, settled on what would work and then either taught others or wrote up the experience for others to study. They were true innovators, venturing boldly where predecessors had taken only tentative steps. Almost all of them were women and usually they had a large institution to sustain them. The men were busy managing the agencies that they had built up. They opened the way, encouraged and sustained the women, and took pride in their accomplishments. It is not easy to think of innovators in other fields—whether in teaching, medicine or social work, who are concentrated in a few decades—who changed an institution the way this company developed the public library. Their achievement deserves more credit than is bestowed in these brief sketches.

### Sarah B. Askew (1863–1942)

While new services were being started within libraries, other pioneers were promoting library service throughout their states. Askew did so in New Jersey, where she became head of the library commission in 1905. On a visit to Cleveland she came under the influence of William Brett, the Director, enrolled in the Pratt Library School, joined the Cleveland staff, and in time became a branch librarian. In 1905, at age forty-two, she moved to the headship of the New Jersey commission. She promptly took her horse and buggy into every part of the state: there were 66 libraries when she started and 316 by 1940. She also pushed county libraries and got twelve underway. During World War I she promoted libraries in army camps and army hospitals. A small woman, she had a strong personality and was an adroit politician. Askew can stand as a model for the many state workers across the country who were the advance agents of the library movement.

### Augusta Baker (1911–98)

Augusta Baker did not originate library service to children but she gave it a fresh richness with her use of storytelling and folklore. She started as children's librarian in the Countee Cullen branch in New York City. There she organized reading clubs and brought in artists and writers. Her skilled storytelling inspired other children's librarians to adopt this technique. She also advanced the cause of literature about Negroes and Negro life with her publications: *Books about Negro Life for Children* and *The Black Experience in Children's Books*. She ended up as coordinator of children's service in the New York Public Library. In 1980, Augusta Baker was storyteller in residence at the University of South Carolina.

**Alice M. Farquhar (1884–1950)**

Alice Farquhar followed a typical career pattern among these early innovators. After completing college, she joined the Chicago Public Library and served as branch librarian from 1913 to 1923. The emerging reader's advisory service caught her interest and she organized and headed the Reader's Bureau in Chicago. By the late 1920s she had adult readers advisers at the central library and in various branches. She was deeply interested in the adult education movement and promoted this specialty in articles in the professional literature. Her "Organization Plan for Adult Education in a Public Library," in J. M. Chancellor's *Helping Adults to Learn* (American Library Association, 1939) made a definite impact. Like others in this small gallery, her focus was upon readers, on their motivations, abilities, and successes and failures as readers.

**Jennie M. Flexner (1882–1944)**

Flexner went to the early library school at Case Western Reserve University (again the influence of William Brett), started in the Louisville Public Library, and shortly became head of circulation. She immediately eliminated the closed shelves. She demonstrated the possibilities of this service in her 1926 book, *Circulation Work in Public Libraries*. Moving to the New York Public Library, she became head of the Readers Advisory Service in 1928. Flexner developed this relatively new service which dealt one on one with motivated readers. She compiled lists of readable books and recommended readings to study groups. Flexner was a lively speaker and was much in demand at group meetings and book reviews. As one source put it, "she died before the tide against formal advisory service," a reference to the elimination in many libraries of this expensive service during the depression and its absorption into the reference function, where it took a backseat.

**Anne Carroll Moore (1871–1961)**

Another graduate of the early Pratt Library School, Moore first became head of children's service at the Pratt Institute Free Library and then went on (1906) to become supervisor of children's work in the New York Public Library. She built the service over the next decades, acquiring collections for young readers and abolishing age limits in their use. She created the position of "children's librarian" and organized Children's Book Week. Her particular interest was in studying children, how they approached books, and what reactions they had to different stories—again, that focus upon recipients as well as upon books. Moore was a recognized newspaper reviewer of juvenile books. No one person can be given credit for starting children's service in public libraries, but Anne Carroll Moore was near the head of the pack.

**Effie Louise Power (1873–1969)**

Here is another of the innovators in children's service; the burgeoning field attracted ambitious recruits who had an empathy with young readers. Power opened a children's room in Cleveland, this back in 1898 when Brett was expanding the Cleveland Public Library. By 1920 she was director of Work with Children in the institution. She was a lecturer in library schools and stressed an understanding of children and the educational process. One reason why juvenile services expanded so rapidly and solidly was the emphasis by the early leaders on understanding the reading process of their particular clientele, a skill that was never acquired by colleagues serving adults. Effie Power joined the faculty of the Columbia Library School in her later years, where she continued her special contribution of training children's librarians. Her 1930 publication *Library Service for Children* set forth the basics of this branch of library service.

**Frances Clark Sayers (1897–1989)**

Sayers is another of the early promoters of children's service. She began her work in Pittsburgh and in 1941 went on to the New York Public Library, where she succeeded Anne Carroll Moore as superintendent of Work with Children. Along the way she wrote several children's books. Another fine storyteller, she was consultant to the Library of Congress. Sayers also followed the pattern of several of the early children's innovators by teaching in library schools, in her case at the University of California both in Berkeley and Los Angeles. The missionary spirit prompted the innovators to bring more and more recruits into the children's fold. Those who were attracted did not often become directors of larger libraries, but they did find much personal satisfaction in their careers, for they could feel the constructive influence they had on young readers.

**Margaret C. Scoggin (1905–1968)**

Scoggin tried to do for teenagers what others had achieved for younger children and to an extent she succeeded. She was superintendent of Work with Young People in the New York Public Library. Scoggin had a secret in dealing with young people: listening instead of telling. Among other accomplishments she started the Nathan Straus branch for this age group. The young people responded to her group activities: clubs, plays, puppet shows, and music programs. Most distinctive were book reviews by the teenagers, reports which were actually put on radio. Scoggin also taught other young adult librarians in the training class of the New York Public Library. Various libraries tried the same service, usually without as much response. Over the years this level of service has hung on and has a body of faithful advocates, but teenagers are simply not as easy to reach as younger children.

**Rose L. Vormelker (1895–1970)**

Vormelker (known as "the businessman's librarian") developed business and technical service first in Detroit and then in

Cleveland. She also had experience in special libraries in business organizations. Vormelker was an advocate of subject specialization in public libraries, which she saw as a means of giving greater depth to reference service. She participated in business and related organizations, for example, the American Statistics Association and the American Marketing Association, and she promoted libraries within business and manufacturing firms. Like others of the innovators, she wrote widely and taught in library schools in order to spread the gospel. She wrote that reference service is producing information "which is needed, at the time when it is needed, and in the form in which it is needed, and in a manner which inspires confidence and respect for the librarian on the part of the user."

## Notes

1. Daniel J. Boorstin, *The Democratic Experience*. (New York: Random House, 1973), 157.
2. George Mowry, *The Urban Nation* (New York: Hill and Wang, 1981), 42.
3. Dee Garrison, *Apostles of Culture: The Public Librarian and the American Society, 1876–1920*. (New York: Free Press, 1979), 242.
4. Lowell A. Martin, *The Optimum Size of Public Library Units* (Ph.D. diss., University of Chicago, 1945).
5. Margaret Monroe, *Library Adult Education: The Biography of an Idea*. (Metuchen, N.J.: Scarecrow Press, 1963).
6. Miriam Braverman, *Youth, Society, and The Public Library* (Chicago: American Library Association, 1979).
7. Ibid., 242.
8. Mary K. Chelton, *Excellence in Library Services to Young Adults* (Chicago: American Library Association, 1994).
9. Robert D. Leigh, *The Public Library in the United States* (New York: Columbia University Press, 1950),100.
10. Maxine M. Merriman, *Augusta Baker: Exponent of the Oral Art of Story-Telling* (Ph.D. diss., Texas Women's University, 1983).
11. Barbara B. Rollock, *Public Library Services for Children*. (Hamden, Conn.: Library Professional Publication, 1988), 4.
12. Enoch Pratt Free Library, *Annual Reports*, 1925 and 1929.
13. Emily Danton, *Pioneering Leaders in Libraries*. (Chicago: American Library Association, 1953).
14. Dee Garrison, *Apostles of Culture*, 173.
15. Ibid., 173–241.
16. Charles C. Williamson, *Training for Library Service*. (Boston: Marrymont Press, 1923).

# 4

# Depression and War, 1930–1945

Herbert Hoover was an able man with a distinguished record when he came into the presidency in 1929. He had headed war relief in Belgium and been secretary of commerce under Harding. But the panic of 1929 and the subsequent depression were too much for him. By the early thirties there were 12 million unemployed (the figure moved up to 17 million a year or two later), and both farms and banks were failing. With his firm belief in market forces and as little government intervention as possible, Hoover did little to stem the tide, and he issued periodic predictions that all would be well in a few months.

Franklin Delano Roosevelt came to office at the bottom of the Great Depression in 1933 and with a different philosophy and attitude. On his first day in office he declared a bank holiday which stopped the run to remove savings from the banks. Roosevelt was a paradox: the product of an estate on the Hudson River and a graduate of Groton and Harvard, yet he maintained touch with the common people and was a consummate communicator with them—"All we have to fear is fear itself." Paralyzed from the waist down, he still came across as a vigorous and congenial man, with a cigarette holder cocked at a rakish angle. This was Roosevelt's decade, and also unfortunately the war that followed is part of his heritage.

Roosevelt's New Deal was essentially human pump priming. This included huge public works, the Civilian Conservation Core, the National Industrial Recovery Act, aid to the poor, even a program for artists and authors. Each of these gave people a hand up or a push, with the aim of individual security and social stability. There were also more permanent projects: Social Security (1935) to provide for retirement years; and the Tennessee Valley Authority (1933), to promote development for a region.

Not that these measures erased the depression in a year or two, however, distressing conditions continued through much of the thirties. One remembers the period in part from Dorothea Lange's realistic photographs of men selling apples, people in a bread line, hungry children, and migrant mothers. Men were hired for ten cents an hour; it is worth noting that Henry Ford, to his credit, supported a wage of five dollars a day. Because wealth had been maldistributed in the 1920s, some people weathered the storm while others came close to starvation.

Roosevelt's measures were not universally approved and supported. On the contrary, for a part of the population he was one of the most hated and vilified of our presidents. With his welfare programs and his aggressive federal government action he opened a division in American civic values that persists to our day, with government activists pitted against free-market advocates. Then his effort to pack the Supreme Court with judges more favorable to his views was not popular. A biographer who favored him wrote that Roosevelt "always cast his vote for life, for action, for forward motion, for the future."[1] His detractors would have used very different language.

Something in the American spirit held the country together in crisis. Men went off on conservation projects; women economized as never before. Every vacant lot had a victory garden. This spirit prevented revolution and slowly turned the country around.

In the course of the century, the only first lady to pursue a career of her own during the years her husband was president and after he died, was Eleanor Roosevelt. She was the mother of six children. She assisted her husband in his political campaigns and advised him on social issues. She was the champion of the underprivileged and minority groups, and she worked persistently for human rights by means of newspaper columns, lectures, and projects. In 1945, after FDR died, she was appointed as the U.S. delegate to the United Nations and she became head of the Commission on Human Rights. In the process Eleanor Roosevelt contributed to the status of women.

Book publishing languished in the early part of the decade but picked up in the midyears. Indeed, the late 1930s brought an outpouring of creative power, some in the popular vein, some as social commentary, and some probing into the human soul.

In 1936 Margaret Mitchell's *Gone With the Wind* was published and sold 1 million copies in the first year. Dale Carnegie's *How to Win Friends and Influence People* did almost as well. Proletarian authors appeared: John Steinbeck, James Farrell, Clifford Odets. Richard Wright issued *Native Son* and John Dos Passos *U.S.A.* Pearl Buck took us to the Chinese countryside, William Faulkner created an imaginary county in which human motives were exposed, and Eugene O'Neill invited us on a *Long Day's Journey into Night*. All three authors would receive the Nobel Prize in Literature. People even found works to suppress: *Ulysses, Jurgen, Sister Carrie, Memoirs of Hecate County*, and some libraries went along. Paperback books appeared and were an immediate success.

With the depression just behind and the war just ahead, a multitude of optimistic songs swept the country: "Oh, What a Beautiful Morning," "You'll be So Nice to Come Home to," "Some Enchanted Evening," "As Time Goes By." A romantic movie, *Casablanca,* won the Academy Award. As the war came on, people even kept their sense of humor and chuckled over the two grimy men in the trenches: "Just gimme the aspirin; I already got the Purple Heart."

The European war opened in 1939 with Germany advancing rapidly both west through the low countries and France and east through Poland and into Russia. Clearly, complete European conquest and the defeat of Great Britain were the goals. At home in Germany, the Holocaust was launched to eliminate the Jews.

Franklin Roosevelt was elected for a fourth term in 1944. He attended the Yalta Conference in February 1945, and died of a cerebral hemorrhage two months later, at 63 years of age. He was the most charismatic figure to appear in this history.

## Overview of Library Development, 1930–1945

The period from 1930 to 1945 proved to be an unplanned test of the public library. The institution had moved forward in the

1920s, enriching its service program, reaching more people, and gaining additional financial support.

Now, like other institutions, the agency faced a double blow, first severe depression and then prolonged war. Were its roots in society deep enough to withstand these blows? Would the public library survive in poor years for the nation—or was it an institution for good times alone?

Library budgets were cut during the depression, book purchases were curtailed and salaries reduced. But the whole economy sank so low. Prices for books and for other commodities fell so far that it was possible to survive on reduced budgets, although at a lower standard—paperback books in place of hardcover, for example, and reduced hours of service. Not many librarians went on the unemployment lines, although staffs were not increased in numbers. In most installations, life went on as before. Staffs were not severely depleted by conscription in the war years, for the majority of library employees were women.

Further, the public library was able to endure because—to the surprise even of its own directors—demand for its materials continued and in some respects increased. People thrown out of jobs turned to the library to learn about alternative possibilities and then to develop whatever background and skills were required for a change. The fact that few were successful in starting a new career did not lessen the effort. There was also self-education needed to cope with straitened circumstances, whether to learn about more economical meals or home vegetable gardens, preserving, or canning. Demand for books about automobile repair and even about raising poultry increased. In a sense small, private home industries were created and the local entrepreneurs needed information on how to proceed. Libraries reported an increase in the proportion of their home circulation made up of nonfiction books.[2]

People who previously purchased their books and magazines discovered the community resource. If all else failed, there was the library as a refuge for a few hours, warm and with a range of reading for diversion, and there was no charge. The statistics of use did not increase but in many localities stayed about the same. The public library added to the basic balance and stability of the American people that carried the country through hard times.

On some fronts progress was actually made during the depression. In larger cities subject specialists were added to the staffs; they could not get employment elsewhere and libraries did not have to budget large salaries to hire them. Librarians strengthened their position on intellectual freedom, resisting pressures from radical fringes. And the search continued for an adequate organizational base in larger governmental units of service.

The same case of substantial use and enhancement of service could not be made for the war years, at least not at first. Men went to war and women went to work in factories. For a period the public library marked time. People not directly affected by the war still came to the agency, and both Red Cross groups and air-raid wardens used the buildings.

Then, after the first years of war, attention shifted to the future. Individuals made plans and post-war planning became the fashion; business, industry, governmental units, and organizations all tried to predict coming conditions and set down their own intentions. Business people in particular consulted library materials. Men discharged from the war and considering returning to school under the G.I. Bill sought to refresh their backgrounds. Then there were the many young children born during and just after the conflict.

If the public library was wounded during the war, it recovered quickly and was whole and sound so it could benefit from a time of revival and economic expansion of the economy in the 1950s.

## Intellectual Freedom

At the turn of the century, most library administrators saw their role as one of protecting their readers from invidious and immoral literature. They reflected the value system of families and communities of the time. The theme of the 1895 annual conference of the American Library Association was "Improper Books: Methods Employed to Discover and Exclude Them." Most speakers railed against improper books, showing no recognition that they were imposing their own personal standards and essentially engaging in censorship. No doubt their honest conviction was that good reading begets good behavior and that what they saw as bad reading would undermine proper behavior and indeed harm the whole community. One librarian offered his solution to the problem: he admitted some objectionable publications for which there was a demand, but attached a note to them warning the patron against reading the item because it did not meet proper standards.

The matter was debated in the first years of the century, as some professional voices were raised against excluding books because they were outside the mainstream. The seed of what was to become the intellectual freedom stance of librarianship was planted, but the plant was a slow grower.

The United Sates was drawn into the First World War and militant patriotism gripped the country—including librarians. The distinguished head of the children's service in the New York Public Library, Anne Carroll Moore, argued in May 1917 that recent attempts by peace organizations to stimulate the writing of peace literature for children should stop. The equally distinguished vice director of the Cleveland Public Library, Linda Eastman, declared that the neutrality of the library should be abandoned and that the agency ". . . had its own contribution to make toward the winning of the war."[3]

British propaganda designed to bring the United States into the war was regularly stocked by public libraries. On the other hand, when we were in the conflict, many libraries—not a few, but many—proceeded to remove titles advocating peace and also any titles by German authors. (One hopes they stopped at Johann Goethe). After recounting pages of examples of such "deselection," the historian who has looked most closely at the problem concluded that "the American public library community clearly failed to resist censorship during World War I."[4]

There were exceptions who stood against the hysteria. John Cotton Dana, the director of the Newark Public Library, who has figured earlier in our story, resisted a concerted effort by a local committee, called the Vigilantes, to get books removed from the library. He said; "I came to the conclusion many years ago that liberty of thought is a very desirable thing for the world and that liberty of thought can only be maintained by those who have free access to opinion."[5]

Such voices came to prevail in the two succeeding decades. Once the war years were past, librarians to some degree coalesced around the doctrine of freedom from bias and of open opinion in building library collections; the public library was to be the place—really the only place in the community—where one could examine both sides of an issue and indeed get access to contrary and unpopular views. The self-examination by the emerging profession was one of its auspicious efforts, and it was to establish a doctrine that would be supported through the rest of the century. And, controversial as this position was, it was over time to gain wide support in the general population.

But this did not prevent some individuals and organizations from protesting some of the material provided, nor on the other hand did it prevent others from proposing and pushing ideas and viewpoints which they advocated. The library was trying to present a balanced collection and to stock material on both sides in controversial matters. But interest groups wanted their particular slant or interpretation emphasized. This might be a political view, a science theory, or a religious doctrine. Why do we have books that describe communism, some critics asked? What about more for one or another political party? Were the positions of labor unions properly represented? Why include material critical of business methods and interests? Don't have publications espousing Darwinian evolution, or its opposite Biblical interpretation. And most pointedly, why not get rid of the material that goes too far on sex?

Protests and pressures came from all sides. This was a problem that could have undermined the public library by building up opposition groups one by one and thus weakening public support for the institution. The response of the library profession was firm and consistent, and won out in the end.

The position of the American Library Association and of most of the profession was first set forth in the Library Bill of Rights of 1939. The document was shortly revised and by the 1948 version made its main points succinctly:

> Books and other library resources should be provided for the interest, information, and enlightenment of all people of the community the library serves. Materials should not be excluded because of the origin, background, or views of those contributing to their creation. Libraries should provide materials and information presenting all points of view on current and historical issues. Materials should not be proscribed or removed because of partisan or doctrinal disapproval.[6]

The Library Bill of Rights was revised and extended in 1948, 1967, and 1980. Why the frequent changes? Because pressures for including or excluding certain materials continued and those promoting intellectual freedom sought to respond to the new challenges.

One such threat came with the prospect of "labeling." Some protest groups, after trying to get material removed from the collection or put on closed shelves, proposed putting labels on the items to which they objected. The label was designed to warn potential readers against the content and might also include suggestions for alternative sources. Libraries recognized this as a form of censorship and most resisted the practice. The protesters stood against the institution and the local librarian and local library board. Persistence on the part of the librarian usually won out; the profession stood firm while the protesters grew weary. The American Library Association stated "Labeling is an attempt to prejudice attitudes and as such, it is a censor's tool."[7]

Then there was the issue of putting some materials on closed or restricted shelves, a practice rather widely practiced by public libraries when objections were raised to particular publications. There was the issue of protecting children against what some parents considered to be undesirable material. The association opposed such restrictions. The library was open for all, and any control would have to come from the parents themselves.

The association put considerable resources into the fight. An Intellectual Freedom Committee was established and an Office for Intellectual Freedom. In time the *Intellectual Freedom Manual* was issued to guide librarians on how to meet the threats. They were urged to get the bill of rights adopted by their boards of directors as policy for the agency, and to do so before an actual protest was in hand. If this should be put off until the emotional feelings of an actual controversy prevail, some individual board members may waver in their position. Many public libraries—but not all—did adopt the policy statement and found it an asset when challenged on their book selection choices.

Challenges to intellectual freedom did not end during war times, whether hot or cold. Late in the century, in the 1990s, very conservative religious groups complained about material that did not support their view of family values. The particular concern is literature that deals with homosexuality, and particularly whether this is a natural or acquired trait. The controversy continues to this date.

While most librarians have tried conscientiously to adhere to the goal of intellectual freedom as conceived by the profession, special conditions have tested them severely. In wartime, should librarians remove books on explosives, as the federal government requested in World War I? What about published material protesting war activities—say in Vietnam—or advising possible recruits to avoid the draft? Then there is the sensitive area of religion. What about polemics against certain faiths, or tracts promoting atheism? There are publications critical of democracy, way back to Plato and before. Most librarians would stand firm against efforts to ban such books. But how far would they go? Would they defend publications that claim that black people are mentally inferior to whites? The challenges multiply and come from many sources and directions.

The strategy of many librarians has been to avoid extreme radical pronouncements on any subject. One can still provide views on each side of a controversy without reaching to the fringe. Or if pressure becomes too insistent, there is the old tactic of removing material from the open shelves until protests have quieted down.

But the truth is, some librarians have simply avoided purchasing titles that might be questioned. A certain number of libraries did not acquire Nabokov's *Lolita* when it first appeared, and then later made the purchase when community standards had moved to the point where such expressions were accepted. Today it would not be easy to avoid all material with sexual content, because many novels purposely include titillating scenes in order to boost sales.

What about the other side of the equation? In book selection, librarians regularly reject publications as not suitable to their collections. Is this a form of self-imposed censorship? If the rejection is prompted by the selector's disagreement with the content, then the answer would be affirmative. But if the librarian holds to the principles of the Library Bill of Rights—material to be chosen for "values of interest, information, and enlightenment," in order to present "all points of view concerning the problems and issues of our times," and not excluded because of "our own political or aesthetic views"—selection becomes appraisal, not censorship.

In a recent interview, Judith E. Krug, for many years head of the Office for Intellectual Freedom of the American Library Association, gave a somewhat surprising answer to the question "What would you say was the biggest threat to intellectual freedom that you have encountered?"[8] Her answer was "ourselves." She was referring to librarians who gave in and censored material, and also to librarians who failed to educate their boards and the general public on the basic value of intellectual freedom. The fight against censorship, while primarily directed against groups in the general public, has also been directed against librarians who sought to avoid trouble by excluding publications to which there are objections.

No doubt there have been librarians who gave in or compromised in the face of challenges to the Library Bill of Rights, perhaps more often than has come to light. But, by and large, the library profession has supported the concept of intellectual freedom, and in the end this has strengthened rather than weakened the image of librarians and of the institutions they maintain.

## Subject Specialization

Public library collections usually include the whole spectrum of subjects, from A to Z, from astronomy to zoology. Without division by subject, librarians typically review publications in these and many other fields and make selections as to what to purchase. Other librarians sit at reference desks and try to handle inquiries over this same wide range. The whole world is out there and inevitably persons from anywhere along the line turn to the agency. The general library is like a department store with the same staff handling everything from women's clothing to hardware.

When staff is small, there is hardly any other alternative for the library. The librarian does have access to a bibliographic apparatus, which supplies the background and judgment of experts, but this is a vast panoply in which different staff members differ widely in their ability to negotiate. Even in libraries without subject specialization, certain staff members come to be recognized as having greater knowledge of history, art, science, or business, depending on their academic backgrounds.

Special staff positions, based on subject fields, appeared in larger libraries even in the 1920s, and then also in the 1930s despite constricted budgets. They continued to appear in the more prosperous period after World War II. There was a rationale behind this development that drove it forward. In substance it provided specialized staff within the framework of general libraries.

The topics selected for specialization were dictated by the various needs of the community. Local history was one of the first to appear, and then art or art-music positions. Business might follow. Specialties were being added to the functional base of acquisition, cataloging, and reference, and is diagrammed in Figure 1.

A special division devoted to business was one of the early specialties. Actually such a service was originated by John Cotton Dana in the Newark Public Library in 1904, and business units spread in the 1920s to libraries in Philadelphia, Cleveland, San Francisco, etc. By the 1930s there were thirty-one business units in larger libraries.[9] These might be a department in the main building or a separate branch in the business district. A collection covering manufacturing, finance, markets, administration, personnel, and related topics was assembled. Part of the literature of business and industry was unlike that of other fields, as in daily stock reports, specialized journals, and annual company reports.

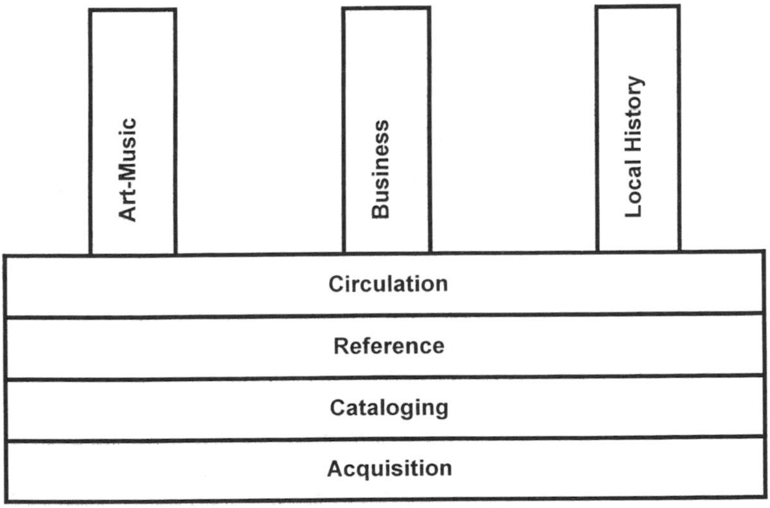


*Figure 1* Emergence of Subject Departments in Public Libraries

Some units even added fiction for business people. Staff members were assigned who had some background in business and economics. They were prepared to serve an influential body of patrons who became an asset as city libraries made requests for financial support.

In time, in larger central buildings, a complete circle of subjects appeared, so that each area of interest had its special staff. This is pictured in Figure 2. The first city agencies to complete the circle were the Cleveland Public Library and the Los Angeles Public Library. The number of subject divisions in the full development is usually six to eight, those shown in the diagram being the original departments in the trend-setting Enoch Pratt Free Library in Baltimore. The Baltimore plan was easy to understand and use. The patron came in at ground level and after a few steps was in a large central hall around which the whole library was visible. By turning on one's heel, the circle of subject and reference departments could be seen. The card catalog was in the central hall, and also directly in front of the entrance a quick-reference and

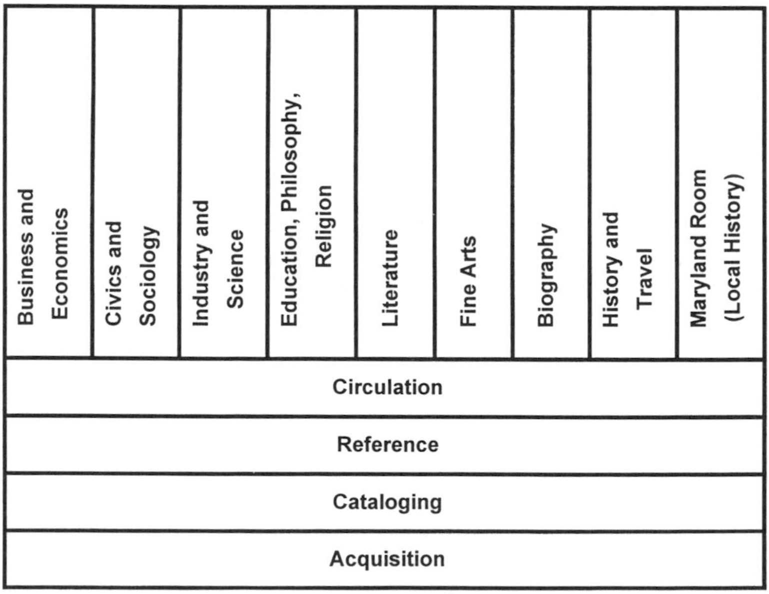


*Figure 2* Full Circle of Subject Departments (Original Plan for Enoch Pratt Free Library)

referral station. Small wonder that other central libraries built in the following years adopted variations of the plan.

The specialized staff positions often grew into departments, where materials in the field were assembled—not just books but also journals, reports, and later audio and visual media. The user had a location suited to his or her interest, staffed by an individual who was knowledgeable in the field. Both across the service desk and in outside meetings with community groups, the specialized librarian and user shared a common background.

Subject specialists sometimes took over from the general staff, by virtue of their knowledge of resources. They participated in book selection, they handled reference questions on referral, and they settled difficult questions in cataloging and classification. In some cases the general reference division becomes more of a catchall for journals, a small reference collection, and in time for microforms. Much of the business goes on in the subject departments.

But this promising development was not without its problems. First, this is an expensive type of organization. Subject librarians command higher salaries than general librarians. Staff with special background in science, technology, and economics are not easy to obtain. Some resources are needed in all the subject rooms and must be duplicated. Separate rooms or divisions must be staffed even if the volume of use at times may not justify it.

As time went on, additional problems appeared. Because it was often difficult to locate subject specialists in some fields who also had library training, staff members with limited subject background were assigned. As a result one of the advantages of subject specialization was lost. Also these specialists were less likely to go out into the community to meet with subject groups. Another concern was their reluctance to physically handle journals and nonprint media, so the task was shifted back to clerical units handling nonbook acquisitions for the whole library.

From the user's standpoint the subject divisions are a convenience for some but not for others. For more casual readers the circle of special rooms may be intimidating. A study of the Enoch Pratt Free Library showed that 51 percent of users had to use two or more departments to satisfy their quests.[10]

Readers working within subject fields as defined by the library have a special collection and staff at their command. But the interests of many people—in such areas as war and peace, environment, social trends, family affairs—spread across neat subject lines. Rather than being helped, users may be confused and find themselves shunted from department to department.

Given these several considerations, some central-city libraries have more recently sought to reduce the number of subject departments. Enoch Pratt did so after the study previously cited. Atlanta built a new structure with just four subject divisions. Rochester, which had copied the Enoch Pratt plan, also reduced the subject units in a new building opened in 1997.

Subject specialization has added depth to public-library service. At the same time, decisions forced by the dollar sign have taken their toll. The concept has intensified content-oriented rather than user-oriented provisions. But it is still needed in a period of increasing specialization and of publication and data overload.

One short-lived variation on subject specialization is worth noting. In the 1940s and 1950s the idea of "interest groupings" was advanced and tried in some locations (for example, Detroit and Chicago). The concept was to group materials not by standard subject categories (a content-oriented approach) but by predominant public interests (a user-oriented approach). Examples were current social problems, personal relations, community affairs, family concerns, leisure-time activities, career development, etc. Materials from various parts of the standard classification, for fiction as well as nonfiction, and in whatever form, were brought together. There is some evidence that the organization stimulated use, but the concept was abandoned as interests changed and it was found that this unorthodox plan impeded students following traditional subject categories.

But where larger libraries can afford it, subject specialization in some form is maintained and represents another step forward in service. When seeker and subject librarian come together and exactly the right material is found, one sees communication resource service at its best.

## Library Buildings and Architecture

A kind of paradox marks library building design in the depression and prewar years. Although the number of new buildings constructed declined in these years, the basic design plan for larger public libraries emerged in this same period.

In the early decades of the century, monumental structures were stressed, what can be called temples or classical showpieces—"mausoleums," one critic called them.[11] They were more a tribute to civic pride than functional structures for library service. The exterior showed up well in a photograph and was impressive from the street. A broad staircase led to the entrance. Examples are the main building of the New York Public Library in Manhattan (1911) and the Free Library of Philadelphia (1927). They stood in contrast to the more forthright and functional department stores being erected nearby.

Inside there was likely to be another staircase, with reading rooms higher in the building. Few people used the interior staircase because elevators were common by this time, and patrons waited at the elevator while the stairs stood empty. In San Francisco's first main public library building the staircase was a favorite resting place of street people. In Chicago the library's colorful tile staircase was the main reason historical preservationists wanted to prevent renovation of the outdated structure. The result was long years of makeshift arrangements and eventually the construction of a new building elsewhere. The nineteenth-century building is used to this day for miscellaneous activities and exhibits, still intact with its tile staircase.

In the early decades of the century a large, central reading room was favored. Both the architect and the librarian envisioned a monumental room with a high ceiling, attention to decorative elements, and long rows of reading tables. Here is where visitors would be taken; here is where readers would be impressed. All this was a legacy from the earlier buildings constructed both in American cities and universities in the great national libraries of Europe.

The main reading room's walls of bookcases could hardly hold the collection of a large library. Book stacks were required. Where to locate the stacks—in the middle, to the rear, in a tower, below ground? All of these alternatives were used. Consequently there had to be a delivery desk, where readers submitted their requests. Pages then went along the rows in the stacks and retrieved the requested material. This was an expensive system and it kept readers and books separate, violating the open-shelf concept.

This brings us again to the Enoch Pratt Free Library building constructed in 1933. Although all the features of this general design plan did not originate in any one building, the Baltimore plan showed how various elements could be incorporated into a simple basic design. Joseph L. Wheeler, the director at Pratt, and architect Alfred M. Githens got together to work out a plan for the new building. The structure has a range of display windows across the front. The entrance is at ground level and leads directly to a central area (not a reading room) with a quick-information desk in the center, the catalog along the rear wall, and with space to the side for charging and discharging books. These form the hub of the edifice. The concept behind the quick-information desk in the center is that ready-reference inquiries can be handled here (a small collection of reference books is readily at hand) while more complex questions are referred to the subject rooms.

Around the central hub, on the same floor, are a circle of subject areas covering the several main fields of knowledge. The user can stand within a relatively few feet of the entrance and locate the range of subject areas in the library. The subject areas are separated from each other not by walls but by freestanding stacks which can be moved as demand in particular areas increases or decreases. Pratt originally had seven areas around the perimeter—education, economics, sociology, science, history, biography, and literature—plus a "popular library" with fiction and current bestsellers.

The book stacks within the rooms held the more commonly used books in each field, and the remainder of the collection (1.6 million items) was on the floor below. With this arrangement the reader, table area, books, and specialized subject staff member were all in close proximity. In addition there was a general reference room holding information sources, newspapers, back issues of journals, and other periodicals. There was some opposition to the new pattern, because it made a library into a department store and lost the inspiring character of the monumental reading room. However, this position flew in the face of the general trend toward a public library that was a populist institution for all the people.

The Pratt plan was copied in other new buildings (for example, in Rochester, New York, in 1937), but in practice it had disadvantages. One was the expense of staffing a half dozen or more subject rooms. Later buildings following the plan tended to have fewer subject rooms. Staff members had to fetch materials from the downstairs stacks when little-used items were requested. Finally, while the Pratt plan is internally flexible it is not easy to add to the building's total capacity—either for books or readers. It is a complete and finished capsule which cannot readily be expanded.

Wheeler and Githens went on to put their ideas and experience in a substantial tome which constituted the guiding reference for a generation or more.[12] The book starts with thirty-three "generally accepted" building principles and covers each step in planning a building, from the interrelation of trustees, librarian, and architect at the start, to the selection of furniture at the end. Each type of room is analyzed. The treatment is detailed and practical, with emphasis on traffic and on the location of staff stations to provide surveillance of all public areas.

After the midcentury, as the number of new library buildings increased and as experience with construction was gained, many additional books on library structures appeared. One, by a consultant on many new buildings, is so practical and detailed that the reader almost feels that he has actually gone through the steps of design and completion of a real structure.[13]

The very first Carnegie buildings, constructed before and after the turn of the century, exhibited wide variations in layouts and sometimes very inefficient arrangements. Later plans had to be submitted before Carnegie grants were approved. Thereafter a Carnegie design included "two wings" or a "right-left" floor plan. An outside, centrally located, staircase led into a modest central hall, with a room going off in either direction and perhaps a small book stack to the rear of the center. A staff station inside the entrance provided surveillance of both rooms and could provide both circulation and reference service. Over the years many modifications were added to the wings, particularly to accommodate children. Architects modernized the facade, lowered the entrance to ground level, and added visual interest with window treatments.

Some of the most striking structures of recent decades have been smaller buildings and city library branches. These smaller structures, which weren't expected to house huge book collections, offered opportunity for innovative layouts and designs. Examples of distinctive designs are the Cleo Rogers Memorial Library in Columbus, Indiana, the Shoreline branch in Seattle, and the Mira Mesa branch in San Diego.

One survey of library buildings constructed in the next period, 1946–76, called these next decades the "Golden Age."[14] Another account stresses the break from the past: "In the past twenty-five years (1941–1966) public library architecture has been mainly a revolt against the previous architecture."[15] During these years, modular design was practiced in larger structures, with floor plans laid out in uniform squares or rectangles so that internal adjustments could be made without extensive reconstruction. Service areas were kept to the lower floors and as close to the entrance as possible. Readers and books were interrelated rather than being put into distinctly separate locations. Compact book storage was experimented with in an effort to get more books into less space. Lighting was moved up to twenty to thirty footcandles, often by using fluorescent fixtures. Substantial central buildings were constructed in this period in Miami, Cincinnati, Denver, Seattle, Minneapolis, Dayton, Nashville, and Washington, D.C.

Several large structures have appeared in cities in the 1990s: Chicago (1991), Los Angeles (1993), Denver (1995), Phoenix (1995), San Antonio (1995), San Francisco (1996), and Rochester (1997). Exteriors for the most part are undistinguished and even traditional. One must reach across the border to Vancouver for the creative exterior of Moshe Safdie in the form of a chambered nautilus.

A few of the recent structures (Los Angeles, Phoenix, San Francisco) have been designed around a dramatic central atrium, which may lift the spirit but which also complicates the disposition of books and reading rooms. Even though the former central staircase was pleasing to the eye, it did not contribute much to service. The contemporary atrium merits the same judgment. Service areas are chopped up into both subject areas and theme areas, and are located on several floors. Users may be impressed, but they may be unsure where the material and staff they need are located. The relative simplicity of the earlier Baltimore plan has been lost.

The designers of these recent structures assumed that the public library of the twenty-first century will be a book-centered institution, as it has been in the past. Space is allotted for a bank of networked workstations with access to computerized catalogs, and the Internet. These are the features stressed in newspaper reports. But the bulk of the space is given to housing large collections of printed materials and to locations for "old-fashioned" readers. In the final period of this history (1980–99), I will speculate on whether this assumption is justified or not.

## County Libraries

The great surge of new libraries established before and after the turn of the century created two basic problems in service provision. One after another, cities and towns took the step, resulting in a map that would show centers of service at intervals, mostly where population was concentrated. But what of the spaces between, made up of small villages and rural areas? According to the national plan issued in 1948, 35 million Americans, one-quarter of the total population, lacked public-library service; one-half of the rural residents of the country lacked such a facility.[16]

The second and related problem was the many established libraries with a population or tax base so small that a reasonable standard of service could not be provided. Although one town would create a library and then other small municipalities down the road would follow, no one of them was able to assign much money to the purpose. It was a structure guaranteed to provide inadequate collections, staffs, and services. The problem was similar to that faced by schools, which was solved by the creation of consolidated school districts.

Research was done about what minimum population size was required to provide an adequate tax base for a standard facility that would come up to a reasonable standard.[17] Obviously the answer would depend on what was considered "standard." The first national standards for public libraries were still in the future. If one took as a minimum standard (1) employment of a professional librarian, (2) annual book acquisitions of at least two thousand volumes, and (3) definite and distinct service programs for adults and for children, the answer was approximately a population of 50,000. This would depend on some variables that differ from locality to locality: per capita support of the agency, and flexibility and effort on the part of staff. As the concept of minimum standards of service increased before and after World War II, and as the one dollar per capita annually for financial support came to be accepted, the minimum population size increased to 100,000. This was the figure advocated in the Public Library inquiry in 1950, along with $100,000 in income.[18]

Many town and village libraries did not come up to this level. Library organizers and extension staff members in state libraries therefore came to advocate the county as the governmental base for adequate service, hopefully with all towns and villages included in the unit. The county-library movement propelled the national service program forward, with some of the progress actually occurring in the depression years. This was the result of effort by both state extension workers and leading individuals. "The influence of single individuals in the promotion of high-quality library service stood out as clearly as the role of the state agency in library progress."[19] By 1930, thirty-four states had legislation permitting county libraries. However, only 260 county libraries were in existence, less than 10 percent of the total approved. California had forty-six of these units, and the state went on to be a leader in this category. Sixty years later, in the 1990s, it is sad to see California county libraries starved financially because of tax rate restrictions.

The typical county service plan showed one or more larger towns as centerpieces, with collections large enough to draw users in from the countryside, supplemented by bookmobiles to carry some materials out to villages, schools and crossroads. Branch libraries also were added.

Making materials available to rural residents, farmers, and others was a notable achievement, because these people in the 1930s and after did not have the many information sources and stimulation that were available to city dwellers. Thus the countryside was catching up with the urban centers, bringing the world of knowledge to the side road and the remote farm.

The need for a larger unit also appeared in metropolitan areas. There would be a central city library, and then as the built-up area extended beyond its borders with suburbs, separate libraries would be added. The establishment of public libraries had been, and continued to be, a matter of local action. As a result the problems noted in rural areas also appeared in metropolitan districts:

units of substandard size with unserved areas in between. Again the county base of organization was a possible solution. Some suburban county libraries were organized, as in Cuyahoga County around Cleveland, Dade County around Miami, Los Angeles County around Los Angeles, and Hennipen County around Minneapolis, and even a few city–county combinations, such as Portland, Oregon, and Multnowah County; Atlanta and Fulton County; and Rochester, New York, and Monroe County. But in many metropolitan areas the governmental basis of library organization remained a patchwork, with some strong agencies, some weak agencies, and with unserved stretches in between.

The county base gave a shot in the arm to library coverage. However, not all county libraries were unified, with all municipalities participating in a single program. Some towns resisted joining the county unit, which reduced what each could accomplish. The result in some instances was a city or town library not open to noncenter residents, while down the street in the same center the county headquarters was located, with a fleet of bookmobiles and a collection for out-of-towners. Furthermore, some town–county agencies were unified, but still did not have a sufficient population or tax base to come up to standard. Two-thirds of the 3,000 counties were below 25,000 in population at that time.

Demographics and municipal rivalry affected coverage nationwide. Occasionally two or more counties would combine to create a multicounty library district, but this was not common. If it was difficult to get all the towns and villages within a county to combine into a single library unit, it was more difficult to get two or more counties to do so. The next move forward waited on the "concept of systems" (see the 1946–59 period). This introduced an intermediate level of cooperation and coordination that pulled in most libraries in an area and which did not require individual libraries to give up their autonomy.

A special larger unit developed in the Tennessee Valley Authority (TVA), a federal–state project authorized in 1933 to control floods and produce electricity. The Authority extended into parts of seven states. Three of the states—Alabama, North Carolina, and Tennessee—established regional libraries extending across county lines.[20] Under the general guidance of Mary U. Rothrock, these units achieved a reasonable level of service not possible by local municipalities operating alone. Federal money was a key factor in getting this experiment under way. The TVA libraries demonstrated the potential of regional organization and cooperation. The movement for library systems surfaced again in the 1950s and 1960s.

The movement for larger units in the form of county libraries in the 1930s and 1940s was a step forward in underpinning the public library with an adequate governmental base. However, as we have seen, this only partly solved the problem. The tension and opposition between local pride on the one hand and a sound overall base of organization still prevailed. In the following years, the 1950s and 1960s, we will record the next large step forward, in the creation of systems and networks.

## Graduate Library School—University of Chicago

One of the recommendations of the Williamson report (see the 1918–29 period) was for an advanced professional school that would introduce an element of research and theory into librarianship. The Carnegie Corporation, following up on the earlier work of Andrew Carnegie, created a grant for this purpose in 1932. The Graduate Library School was established at the University of Chicago, where Robert Hutchins welcomed unusual university programs.

The school admitted only graduates of first-year library schools and it awarded the Ph.D. degree. A research-minded faculty was assembled by Louis R. Wilson, who came from a distinguished career as Library Director at the University of North Carolina. The group included Pierce Butler teaching library history, Carleton Joeckel teaching the government and administration of libraries, Douglas Waples from the field of education who devoted himself to the study of reading and library use, and Leon Carnovsky who brought a background in sociology from his service in the St. Louis Public Library. Butler produced his *Introduction to Library Science*, which stressed principles to guide a librarian's practice, and which to this day is still the best introduction to librarianship for a new recruit; Joeckel went on from his work on government to propose a *National Plan for Public Library Service* that was applied in subsequent decades; and Waples published a series of studies on reading, starting with *People and Print* (University of Chicago Press, 1938) and going on to *What Reading Does to People* (University of Chicago Press, 1940), and other titles.

The faculty was a mix of dedicated and independent-minded individuals who often disagreed with each other. Out of their exchanges came some of the probing and challenging articles that began to appear in the professional literature. Doctoral candidates learned, as they approached their final oral examinations, to remain silent when differing faculty members began arguing with each other. Dean Louis R. Wilson, a wise man, supported and coordinated the work of the group.

The Graduate Library School provided a stimulating and heady atmosphere. In the depression decade, when opportunities in the established professions and in business were circumscribed, the school was able to attract outstanding students, most of them doctoral candidates. Once they showed promise, Dean Wilson was ingenious in locating sources of money for fellowships and part-time assignments. Actually more than half of the students were pursuing academic careers and did not come from public libraries, for the Ph.D. degree was recognized more in colleges and universities. Many of the graduates went on to head academic libraries.

But the research interests of faculty members included fields of concern in the public-library sector. Joeckel probed into governmental problems and led a movement for national planning for libraries, Carnovsky concentrated more on analysis of collections and evaluation of services, and Waples sought to lay the foundations of a science of reading. If these various investigations had continued over several decades, public-library administration and service today would be based on a more solid body of principles than actually exists.

The School also had a direct effect on public libraries, holding annual week-long seminars that drew in well-established administrators from the field. The theoretical approach confronted the practical world. It was instructive, for example, to listen to Ralph Munn, the down-to-earth Director of the Pittsburgh, Pennsylvania Public Library discuss issues with Joeckel and Carnovsky.

The *Library Quarterly* was started under the aegis of the school, the first research journal in the field, and for a decade or more a steady stream of critical and research volumes emanated from the University of Chicago Press. The Graduate Library School was noted by the profession, and although no marked changes occurred in practice, fresh questions appeared in library meetings and library publications. The school was watched by the profession but its findings were seldom applied.

Then, just after World War II, the proposal came forth for adding the first year of regular professional study to the curriculum. I sat in on these discussions and remember president Hutchins speaking against losing focus and thinning out the resources of the school by adding more responsibility. He was right. The Graduate Library School lost its special edge, graduated fewer Ph.D.s, and in time was among the first of the established library schools to be terminated, essentially because it did not continue to have the research depth expected of graduate schools at the University of Chicago.

## Notes

1. Arthur M. Schlesinger, Jr., *The Coming of the New Deal*, (Boston: Houghton Mifflin, 1958), 588.
2. Philip A. Kalisch, *The Enoch Pratt Free Library: A Social History*. (Metuchen, N.J.: Scarecrow Press, 1969), 153.
3. Wayne A. Wiegand, *An Active Instrument for Propaganda: The American Public Library During World War I*. (New York: Greenwood Press, 1989), 30.
4. Ibid, 111.
5. Ibid, 96.
6. American Library Association, *Intellectual Freedom Manual*, (Chicago: American Library Association, 1983), 14.
7. Ibid, 32.
8. *American Libraries*, vol. 26 (1995), 774.
9. Marg Birkowski, *An Evaluative Survey of the Literature of Public Library Service to Business, 1925–1962*. (Master's thesis, Catholic University of America), 1965.
10. Lowell A. Martin, *Space in the Pratt Central Building*. 2 in the Deiches Fund Studies (Baltimore: Enoch Pratt Free Library, 1964), 3.
11. Thomas H. Ballard, *The Failure of Resource Sharing in Public Libraries and Alternative Strategies of Service*. (Chicago: American Library Association, 1986), 170.
12. Joseph L. Wheeler and Alfred M. Githens, *The American Public Library Building*. (New York: Scribner, 1941).

13. Raymond M. Holt, *Planning Library Buildings and Facilities: From Concept to Completion.* (Metuchen, N.J.: Scarecrow Press, 1989).

14. A. Robert Rogers, "Library Buildings," in Sidney L. Jackson, ed. *A Century of Service.* (Chicago: American Library Assocation, 1976), 233.

15. Joseph A. McDonald, "Twenty-Five Years of Public Library Architecture, 1941–1966," in *Public Library Architecture.* (Philadelphia: Drexel Press, 1967), 1.

16. Carleton B. Joeckel and Amy Winslow, *A National Plan for Public Library Service.* (Chicago: American Library Association, 1948), 19.

17. Lowell A. Martin, *Optimum Size for Public Library Service.* (Ph.D. diss., University of Chicago, 1945).

18. Robert D. Leigh, *The Public Library in the United States.* (New York: Columbia University, 1950), 155.

19. Gretchen K. Schenk, *County and Regional Library Development.* (Chicago: American Library Association, 1954), IV–V.

20. Patricia C. Smith, *The Tennessee Valley Authority and Its Influence in the Development of Regional Libraries in the South.* (Master's thesis, University of North Carolina, 1954).

# 5

# Recovery and Uncertainty, 1946–1959

Economic recovery proceeded apace after the war and through the 1950s. Yet for many people it was a period of uncertainty—about atomic bombs, about race relations, about sexual behavior, and Johnny's alleged inability to read. Old ways were being challenged. What symbol characterized the 1950s—president Eisenhower or Senator McCarthy, Martin Luther King or Elvis Presley, Billy Graham or Marilyn Monroe, Betty Freidan (*The Feminine Mystique*) or Grace Metalious (*Peyton Place*)?

It was an entertaining time for anyone watching the parade of human foibles.

These were the Truman-Eisenhower years, for the most part orderly years, although it did not take long to get the United States embroiled in another war, this one—of all places—in Korea. Also the Soviet Union and the United States faced each other, both with atomic bombs that could annihilate each other. The Marshall Plan revived Europe and the McArthur policies revived Japan.

Soldiers back from the war continued their education under the G.I. Bill, and then pushed on to "getting ahead," the predominant motive of the time. A culture of consumption was in the driver's seat, epitomized in John Galbraith's *Affluent Society*. Perhaps the shopping mall should be the symbol for the decade.

When cities spread out into the suburbs, dividing metropolitan areas into many communities and governments, it affected libraries as well as other public services. The birth rate mounted; more babies were born from 1948 to 1953 than in the previous thirty years. And the divorce rate went up, revealing the first fissure in the American family. Several million migrants who had come north for jobs during the war were in the cities, some of them creating urban ghettos; this also had its impact on the public library, which would try to reach into the slums. There was a sexual revolution, perhaps more publicized than actually practiced; Albert Kinsey's *Sexual Behavior in the Human Male* was a bestseller despite its dry, impersonal presentation.

Television spread over the land. Night after night families looked at Milton Berle or Lucille Ball or an Ed Sullivan show. TV projected a bountiful American life style, carried forward by advertising. Conformity was the underlying effect. Again we see a relation to the public library, for it is a source of diversity and individuality rather than uniformity.

Some progress occurred in race relations. A first step in desegregation was taken in *Brown* v. *Board of Education* (1954), striking down the doctrine of "separate but equal" in the provision of schools. Martin Luther King Jr. stood up and preached nonviolent resistance. Jackie Robinson and Willie Mays entered the lineups in the baseball's major leagues. But racial prejudice ran deep. One remembers the image of a black girl walking to the door of the school in Little Rock, Arkansas, through a crowd of taunting white adults.

Other fissures appeared in the fabric of American life. As always some independent authors probed and found the trouble spots. Tennessee Williams and Arthur Miller did this in the theater. Sloan Wilson challenged conformity in *The Man in the Gray Flannel Suit* and David Riesman perceived alienation in *The Lonely Crowd*.

The book world recovered with the rest of the economy. Hardcover books published in the United States rose to twelve thousand titles annually. Paperback books sold by the millions. A billion comic books were consumed each year, at a cost of $100 million, four times the book budgets of all public libraries combined. And off in the shadows a new communication and calculating device emerged, called the electronic digital computer.

Who could foretell that reducing data to two binary numbers would create a revolution? We still don't know what this really means for libraries.

Nor was the musical world silent. Jazz was the popular music of the day. Musical productions from *My Fair Lady* to *West Side Story* graced the stage. How can one account for the popularity of Elvis Presley, even to this day? He was not an outstanding singer; he could gyrate, but he couldn't dance; he died of an overdose of drugs. Was it simply that he was a sex symbol?

By the end of the decade the cold war got colder. The Soviets launched Sputnik in 1957, sending a shockwave not only to government officials in the United States but also to the populace in general and to the schools in particular. On the international front the United Nations and the North Atlantic Treaty Organization were formed.

The individual struggled to get ahead, sat back occasionally to consider the dynamic social and technological changes, turned on his television set, and the next morning went back to work. Many careers were available and people joined in what some called "the rat race." Was this the dynamo that Henry Adams had predicted many years before?

## Overview of Library Development, 1946–1959

Having survived depression and war, public libraries had achieved a kind of maturity by midcentury. Significant parts of the innovations of the 1920s had caught on. Public acceptance of the agency had been reinforced and financial support would increase in the 1950s. Seasoned administrators were in place and experienced staff members carried on service day to day. The public library was a viable institution, visible on the main street, in branch locations, in small towns and on country roads.

At the same time it was in a sense a secondary institution, not as prominent as the schools, not as demanding on the public treasury, not as foremost in the public mind. In the next half-century it might become more essential, it might fade into the shadows, or it might continue on its appointed way. The task here is to trace the road that it actually took.

What was done first was self-appraisal. Part of the examination came from the outside in the form of the Public Library Inquiry. Carnegie Corporation money was obtained and a group of social scientists performed the analysis. The results of the inquiry will be reviewed shortly. That there was such an examination and that it was sponsored in part by the American Library Association suggests that there were questions and concerns on the minds of various leaders, and that they sought advice on purpose and direction. The inquiry was a study of some substance, but it did not have a marked impact on library administration, nor did it result in increased investment in public libraries on the part of the Carnegie Corporation. For the most part the profession shrugged off the inquiry.

Librarians themselves also looked inward. National standards were compiled and promulgated to stimulate greater effort on the part of library administrators and government officials. A national plan was published for library service. Efforts were stepped up to gain federal financial aid for public libraries. The 1950s were to be a time of stirring on the part of librarians, in step with the stirring of the nation to gain a strong economy and a satisfying social order.

Efforts were made in these years to raise librarianship to the level of a profession. The standard for a library career became completion of a graduate program of education. The number of graduate library schools increased, as did membership in the American Library Association. Management efforts were made to get more return from professional librarians on the job. Steadily book collections were expanded and deepened. And state library agencies moved more to the front.

It was a period for moving forward. Despite criticisms from within and from the outside, the institution in the postwar years would exhibit growth, durability, and some flexibility. As the country settled into place, so did the public library.

## Appraisal at Midcentury

After the war, the American Library Association requested the Social Science Research Council to make a study of the public library—the Public Library Inquiry was sponsored by the Carnegie Corporation which had promoted public libraries for many years, dating back to the Carnegie building grants. The Carnegie Corporation welcomed an appraisal of its beneficiary. It was to be "an appraisal in sociological, cultural and human terms of the extent to which the librarians are achieving their objectives" and "an assessment of the public library's actual and potential contribution to American society."[1] The project came to be termed the Public Library Inquiry.

The Social Science Research Council selected a political scientist, Robert D. Leigh, to head the inquiry, and he in turn recruited a staff of twenty-four research associates and assistants from the fields of the social sciences. The result was the general report already cited, six published volumes,[2] and several unpublished reports. Methods used included statistical analysis, questionnaires, interviews, and field visits to a sample of sixty libraries.

The inquiry first reviewed the objectives of the public library as stated in the post-war standards and the national plan. The conclusion was that "librarians have been on the right track in describing their purposes."[3] The inquiry tended to put public affairs and citizenship first, which led to a paradox because this objective was not given priority in actual library practice. The report stresses again the great disparity in size and support of public libraries: 2 percent of units serving over 100,000 people and 65 percent serving less than 5,000, with corresponding differences in financial support. The conclusion here is that "the United States has a multitude of libraries, some of them magnificent institutions, but it has no library system."[4]

On this basis, the Public Library Inquiry proposed a concerted move toward larger and combined units, whether by consolidation or by coordinated programs on the part of autonomous libraries. This of course was not an original proposal, because this had been the main thrust of the National Plan which appeared two years before the inquiry report.

The inquiry goes on to appraise the services provided by public libraries. The materials and guidance given to children is termed an "impressive achievement" and a "classic success."[5] As to adult education, "the public library has not become a major center of formally organized adult education under its own initiative."[6] Equally the reference or information function is not given a positive rating, and from a poll the inquiry commissioned it reaches the conclusion that "for many people their library had little significance as a source of information."[7]

The inquiry report took a look at book selection (fairly balanced and objective), at operations (not efficient and cost productive), and personnel (librarians only partly qualify as a profession). It is an analytical account, critical but at the same time sympathetic to the basic mission and accomplishments of the institution.

On this basis the Public Library Inquiry recommends an increase of 50 percent in the public money going into public libraries, this to come in part from federal and state financial aid as well as greater local effort. For a service program which has any chance of achieving the professed objectives, the report says that a minimum budget of $100,000 was needed (which would be three times as large in 1990 dollars).

On the whole the appraisal is positive, and this by a group of social scientists who had little reason to favor the public library and who looked at it objectively. There is little here that broke new ground; most of what the Public Library Inquiry recommends could have been found in other sources, particularly the National Plan of 1948.

## Use and Users

One would think that an agency such as the public library would know about its users—how many there are, who they are, what they come for and, how satisfied they are. One would think that such information would be turned to in every planning session and at budget time. But this was not the case at midcentury, and it still is not the case today.

The one statistic usually kept by libraries is the circulation figure, the number of items charged out for use off the premises. This is relevant because it is one measure of use. But it does not measure all use, for it does not show how many books are consulted inside the library, nor is the circulation figure a count of users, for some individuals take out two or more books. Similarly, the file of registrants is not a reliable source, for it contains the names of individuals who came in once or a few times and may not have returned in a year or more, and it lacks accounting of who came in to consult sources or obtain information and never got into the files.

Some libraries have tried to fill the gap by means of attendance counts taken at the door either by hand or by automatic counters. This obviously told little about who the users were or what they were seeking or their degree of satisfaction or frustration. The circulation figure could be broken down by fiction and nonfiction, and the latter by subject groups, but this was not often done and only reflected use outside the building. A small number of libraries tried to keep counts of in-building use by asking readers to leave publications used on the tables and not return them to the shelves, and then counted the number of volumes before reshelving them. This was not very accurate: however, because individuals would take a half-dozen items to examine before picking one to read. Some libraries kept a tally of number of questions asked at the reference desk, occasionally broken down by directional questions, brief searches, and inquiries requiring three minutes or more to answer.

But even these partial statistics of use were not often studied by administrators or professionals, and some were abandoned after a period. The count at the reference desk was a bother to maintain and the circulation breakdown was less easy to determine when machine circulation came into the picture after mid-century. A few libraries sought to question users when they were leaving to determine whether they had found what they wanted, but this was time-consuming and was also abandoned; libraries do not have even as much data about use as restaurants and retail concerns that ask patrons to fill out evaluation forms. A rewarding method for analyzing library use has not been found, primarily because librarians have simply not been disposed to analyze their patronage and performance.

This is not to say that no studies have been done of public library use and users. We will shortly refer to the analysis done as part of the Public Library Inquiry.[8] The report from the inquiry depended in part on some dozen limited studies, most of which were done after World War II, and the inquiry itself added a statistical survey. A search of the literature since that report turned up a few additional efforts to probe into use and users, but these were few and far between and in most cases based on limited samples; they will be examined after looking at what the Public Library Inquiry found.

In its commission to provide "an appraisal in sociological, culture and human terms of the extent to which the libraries are achieving their objective," the inquiry naturally sought information about use and users. Two separate sources were utilized: a national sample survey of 1,151 interviews by the Survey Research Center of the University of Michigan, and an analysis of a dozen smaller studies done between 1930 and 1947. No claim is made that these sources provide all the data that might be desired.

If one sentence could summarize the study, it would be: "Most adults use the library not at all, some use it infrequently, and a few use it a great deal."[9] "Few" here is 18–25 percent of adults and up to 30 percent of children and young teenagers, depending on the locality and on the source of the data. A large portion of the adult patrons use the agency only at wide intervals and a small portion frequently and intensively. The adult users tend to be younger, better-schooled and culturally alert, as compared with the total population. Some evidence indicates that the users include community and opinion leaders. Use may have been increasing some over the years, and we will later note evidence that this has occurred. In general, users were satisfied with the service received.

Approximately 25 percent of the books read came from the public library at that time (other primary sources were purchases, home libraries, and friends). Consultation of the card catalog was infrequent as were requests for reading guidance. "As a source of information, the public library has little reality for most people."[10]

The findings were not favorable for most proponents of the agency. However, the data were not final nor completely reliable in all cases. Some critics pointed out that the scientific findings simply confirmed impressions that any observant librarian would gain.

Berelson himself proposed that more definitive studies were needed. He posed various analytical questions: How "important" are the people who use the library—why do a few individuals of limited education turn to the agency—what of the falloff in use in the early adult years—who are the users who do not get into either the registration or the circulation figures? He could make no claim that he had determined the social effect of the public library.

Berelson went on to interpret the implications of his findings for library policy. He came down on the side of facing reality and concentrating on the minority who use the library, as against a policy of trying to serve the whole community. Some practitioners criticized him for this "negative" position, and in general public-library policy followed the communitywide concept in the following years, not the concentration on existing users recommended in the inquiry.

In the decades since the Public Library Inquiry, polls of public library use have shown an increasing public response. After a temporary decline in the early 1970s, home circulation of books has moved steadily upward. A Gallup poll in 1995 found that 67 percent of American adults went to a public library at least once during the preceding year, up from 51 percent in 1978— both figures markedly higher than the Public Library Inquiry report of the late 1940s. Most users borrowed books (80 percent), 64 percent used reference materials, and 35 percent checked out records, tapes, or films. These figures would appear to be an indication of the outreach policies followed in recent decades.

In the first half of the century, the public library was established and built a service program that has endured. In the second half of the century the agency expanded and built up a clientele, to the point where any prediction that it will shortly be superseded arouses general disagreement.

A very different question about use and users has to do with the availability of library service to minorities, particularly African Americans. An early study of provision in the South found that in libraries "This dual system has resulted in special difficulties in establishing facilities for the Negro in the first place and in providing anything approaching adequate or equal service in the second place."[11] More than that, many localities did not provide any service at all for African Americans; of a total of 774 public library units in the South, only 99 provided service for Negroes"[12]—this in 1940. In 1930 a survey found that no service was provided for this group in such cities as Columbus, Georgia; Dallas; Jackson, Mississippi; Miami; Mobile, Alabama; and Raleigh, North Carolina;[13] among others.

There were exceptions. The Louisville Public Library established a colored branch as early as 1905. The story hour there attracted upwards of 150 children. In time this unit came to train colored librarians, as other cities, from time to time, decided to take action.

The *Brown* v. *Board of Education* decision of the Supreme Court came in 1954. Based on the equal protection clause of the fourteenth Amendment to the Constitution, this decision struck down the separate but equal concept in the provision of schools and public services. Some southern libraries desegregated voluntarily, others waited for court orders, a few acted after sit-ins, and some actually closed for a period rather than comply. Slow but steady progress was made during the 1960s. This was documented by a research project sponsored by the American Library Association and carried out by International Research Associates, Inc.[14]

The picture in the northern and western states was of course more favorable, with access afforded to minorities from early on. But the study just cited raised a related question, that of "indirect discrimination." This referred to unequal provision, with fewer outlets provided in the low-income areas of cities, and with fewer books and other resources when they were provided. Philadelphia, Detroit, and New York, along with six large southern library systems, were accused of indirect discrimination by locating branches in areas not likely to be used by minorities. "In Philadelphia, a heavily white neighborhood is six times as likely to possess a branch as a predominantly non-white section. In Detroit, twice as many branches are located in heavily white neighborhoods and these branches contain more than one and one-half times as many books as those in predominantly non-white areas."[15] City library administrators objected to this criticism, but there was some evidence to support the accusation.

E. J. Josey pushed the analysis one step further when he analyzed the content of library collections. "Most of our public libraries, including the large metropolitan libraries, provide their readers only material to mirror the white community. In short, black experience is invisible in most library collections."[16] This brings up the question of integration of library staffs, for it is staff members who select the books. A government report[17] found that minorities are not represented on library staffs in nearly the same proportion as in the population as a whole.

In 1996 the American Library Association announced a program for diversity and minority recruitment to the profession.[18] The association hired a staff member to handle the program, raised its minority fellowship positions at headquarters from one to three, and sought to increase the number of scholarships available for minorities to attend library schools. All of this was commendable, but it is worth remembering that racial prejudice has deep roots in individuals inside as well as outside librarianship, and such prejudice is reinforced when white people consider the prospect of minorities in the professional ranks.

When the campaign for extension of federal aid for libraries was underway in the early 1960s, the question arose of whether the original Library Services Act was actually working to perpetuate segregation in the South. After all, there were red bookmobiles for Negroes and blue bookmobiles for whites. A report by Roger McDonough on library service in the South,[19] testified to efforts by library administrators to break down racial barriers. Indeed, library service was seen as a kind of bellweather in moving toward integration.

The public library seeks to reflect the whole of American life. At its best, it progressed over the century from a gentleman's institution to a representation of people high and low. Race relations have improved during this same period, with court decisions, affirmative action, and self-development in black communities, but it would be overly sanguine to say that all racial prejudice has been eradicated.

An intriguing and ironic question arose in the late 1950s, that of service to students. The Soviet Union launched Sputnik in 1957, and the United States responded with increased military preparation and a demand that schools tighten their programs and stress mathematics and science. Students were given more homework and more projects requiring extensive reading and location of information. School libraries were seldom prepared for the onslaught, so the young people turned to the public library. One would think that the agency would welcome them with open arms.

But the public library was not prepared either. Books had not been selected explicitly to support school programs. Nor was the agency physically equipped or mentally prepared to deal with the throng of students, mostly at the high-school level. Soon reports came back that every chair was taken, that collections were wearing out, that adults were discouraged about using the library. One read of the ". . . traumatic encounter with today's school population" or the summary that in the past two or three years, concern has changed to alarm and alarm, in some cases, to near panic."[20] Fortunately, in time school libraries improved and public libraries overcame their panic.

Overall the various examinations of use show the public library in the last half of the century to be extending its base in the population. On its side the institution has been getting closer to the people, and on their side the people appear increasingly to be developing interests which the agency can serve—possibly the result of the steady increase in level of education of Americans as a whole. This bodes well for the future, for the public library will be tested as the society moves towards digitized information and electronic communication.

Studies also show that beyond the users, who naturally appreciate the services, there are many people who believe the public library to be an asset to the community even though they do not go there, and who are willing to see tax money allotted for its maintenance. Assuming that the infrastructure for reading and for information-gathering remain the same as in the past, the institution would appear to be in a solid and comfortable position for entering the tweny-first century. To most people, nonusers as well as users, the public library is seen as a worthy contributor to the quality of life within communities.

## Politics and Libraries

The prosperity of the 1950s provided an opportunity for libraries to gain much-needed financial support. Did they seize the opportunity? Only to a limited extent. The most notable success was at the federal level, with legislation that will be reviewed in the next section covering the 1960s. At the state level, significant financial aid was gained in some states but very little in others. A similar uneven record must be reported at the local level, the source of the main support of public libraries (75 percent or more). Among libraries serving 100,000 people or more, financial support by 1960 ranged from less than $1 per capita to several times that amount.

This uneven record of taking advantage of good times raises the question of political effectiveness of the public library. Public money is gained by entering the political arena and exerting pressure on the powers that be. It is worth standing back to assess the political role and the political acumen of the institution and its officers and advocates.

A warning had been issued at the start of the decade, in one of the reports of the Public Library Inquiry. Oliver Garceau underlined the inevitable relation of public administration and the political process: " public administration at every level is a political process, operating within a matrix of political forces, adjusting to and building on dynamic political change in the community."[21] He went on to give libraries and librarians a relatively low mark in their performance in the political arena. Indeed he accused library authorities of consciously or unconsciously seeking to avoid getting their hands dirty in politics.

Forty years later the same assessment is the recurring theme in an assemblage of articles about libraries and politics.[22] Successful campaigns are analyzed, as carried out by the American Library Association at the national level, some forceful at the state level groups, and grassroots organizations. But one of the participants in the legislative process offers this view: "From my vantage point as a legislator and a trained librarian, I would say that this lack of knowledge of the legislative process on the part of librarian is the major reason for the low priority which libraries hold with legislative bodies."[23] The problem starts with the usual government of the public library by an appointed board of directors. This has insulated the agency from political influences and pressures to a degree. No doubt some favoritism has entered into decisions by local governments as to who was appointed to the library board, but by and large it has been viewed as an opportunity to designate respectable and established local residents. In some cases the appointment is treated as reward for an individual who has been active in community and cultural affairs and who may have some literary bent. This practice has resulted in library boards that are usually respected by the public, and it has also resulted in some trustees who tend to be passive and inactive in dealing with library policies and in any effort to gain financial support for the institution.

Once in office, library board members find that they have relatively little contact with local politics. The state law gives them considerable authority over the agency. Working with the library administrator, they dispose of library business without referring to local political parties or individuals. Government officials on their side are just as pleased to leave the library administration to the boards and the chief librarian, thus relieving them of having to give attention to another service agency. It must be added that most library trustees and library administrators are equally pleased not to have to practice the art of politics. Thus city hall and the library go along their separate ways.

The other side of the coin is that the library has relatively little contact with government when it comes to getting financial support. If an increased budget is proposed, the library has few spokesmen within city hall and the trustees have little political clout. It is usually left to the library administrator to make the case, and he or she has few active supporters. It is unusual for the public to be organized in any way to push the case for the institution.

We will see the effect of a consistent and knowledgeable campaign by the American Library Association in 1950 and 1960 in gaining substantial aid at the federal level. Further effort at this level led to the creation in 1970 of the National Commission on Libraries and Information Science (NCLIS). Composed primarily of lay people, NCLIS is charged with advising the executive and legislative branches of the federal government on library policies, plans, and needs. The group has not exhibited much force, either in the development of national policy for libraries nor more recently as the federal position on information provision and the Internet is being considered.

The value of knowledge of the legislative process and of consistent political pressure is also exhibited in the work of groups in New York State (as one example of successful campaigns in other parts of the country). New York provides more than 80 million dollars annually in state aid for libraries, over $4 per capita. Three-quarters of this goes to public-library systems, with lesser proportions to regional reference and research centers, school library systems and related projects.[24] The state library and the State Library Association have maintained contact with state legislators over the years. A lobbyist is stationed in the state capital. Most members are visited every year and given word about library needs and advances; some members are convinced and take up the cause. As a result the New York legislature has standing subcommittees on libraries in both the assembly and the Senate. The board of regents, under which libraries are organized, places public libraries as well as school and academic libraries on its agenda. When library legislation is introduced, it goes in as a statutory measure, which means that it is not a temporary matter for one or a few years but is a part of state law which can be changed or abrogated only by new legislation. Behind the action in Albany is an ongoing public relations campaign within communities, which gets right down to favorable editorials in newspapers, library messages which appear each morning on the side of the milk carton at the breakfast table, and even pieces in the programs at professional football games. Much of this public relations program is financed by grants from private sources.

Janet Welch has shown how the same principles apply at the intermediate level of multitype library systems.[25] This important level, which improves service by cooperation and coordination among libraries, presents a special problem because these structures do not work directly with the public and therefore cannot readily engender grass-roots support. But by patient work the role and impact of multitype systems can be made clear to legislators, and at a certain point some come to adopt this special facility as one of their own favored programs. If the governor cuts the library aid budget, these legislators step in to correct the situation.

Public libraries, whether they wish it or not, are involved in the political process at the federal, state, and local levels, and with the several branches of government. This is more than an occasional brush with local party politics. Effort must be directed all the way from the White House to city hall. What is needed is two key elements now lacking: a national policy for libraries and active advocates from friends of libraries in all guises.

This may seem like an impossible goal—the library with its place in the political process. But there is a latent foundation of support, in the service of the agency to which few object, and in the appeal of the message once it is articulated.

An extreme example of what can be accomplished is reflected in this opening of an Op-Ed piece in the *New York Times* by a journalist who was a little carried away with his subject:

> Tonight in swank dining rooms up and down Manhattan, the city's ruling class—those ubiquitous celebrities and just-plain-rich people

you can't escape in the style pages and gossip columns—will toast the New York Public Library's 100th anniversary in 100 separate dinners.[26]

The author added that the price of dinner was $350.

## Standards of Library Service

Even before the Allied troops landed in Normandy, the United States was making plans for the postwar years. The country looked forward to recovery and to a quality of life never envisioned before. This would include not just economic recovery but also the enrichment of cultural life, the design of cities, the protection of the environment, and the improvement of schools—and libraries.

At the federal level the effort was spearheaded by the National Resources Planning Board. For libraries, the American Library Association (ALA) joined with the federal board. A three-stage project was devised, starting with the establishment of national standards for libraries, going on to a survey of the existing level of actual service to compare with the standards, and culminating in a national plan to direct efforts in the 1950s and beyond. The five-year project was completed in 1948 with the publication of the plan.[27]

The Post-War standards were compiled by thirty-one committee members and consultants,[28] including practicing librarians, staff members of the American Library Association and library-school faculty members. The document rests on an inclusive list of objectives for the library, from the usual education-appreciation-recreation combination and on to such broad goals as maintaining "the precious heritage of freedom" and preparation for "useful occupations and practical affairs."[29]

The standards themselves are both quantitative and qualitative—more of the latter than of the former. The established $1.00 per capita for financial support is repeated, but with the expansion to $1.50 for reasonably good service and $2.00 for superior service. Many of the numerical standards are quite varied and flexible, depending on local conditions: 3 to 10 volumes circulated per capita per year, 20 to 40 percent of adults registered as borrowers, holdings of 1 to 3 volumes per capita in the collection. The wide variations demonstrate the difficulty of prescribing exact figures for situations as different as Boston and Adams, Massachusetts in the Berkshire hills or as different as Cleveland and the college town of Springfield, Ohio.

The qualitative standards in the document are often more accepted principles of administration rather than standards as such. "The librarian should have a warmth of personality, and should possess those qualities of leadership which mark him as a leader in the educational, cultural and civic life of the community"[30] and "the building should be functional in design, without applied ormentation."[31] In substance the standards amount to a brief primer on administering a public library.

Perhaps the most serious criticism that can be made of the 1943 standards is that they do not address the quality of service. Some of the quantitative statements can be used for this purpose, but they will be interpreted quite differently by different evaluators. How does one estimate the quality of a collection, its relevance, depth, and currency? How does one judge the quality of reference service, its suitability to the particular inquirer? This statement does not help much at this level. The whole subject of measurement and evaluation will be taken up in the 1960–79 period.

None the less, the postwar standards were used to good effect to survey and appraise the general library situation at the end of the war. Data were obtained from the various states and from four hundred libraries reporting to the ALA. The conclusions set down in the second chapter of the Post-War Plan were that 35,000,000 Americans lacked any public-library service, most library agencies were too small to be able to maintain adequate service, and financial support in many localities was so low that provision at best must be rated as mediocre. This is not the first time that we have come on these problems.

The National Plan,[32] which appeared five years later, proposed a drastic restructuring of public libraries in the United States, reducing the total library units from 7,500 to some 1,200. These would be made up of countywide agencies, multicounty units, and larger districts. The comparison was made to the consolidation then occurring in larger school districts to get away from limited one-room schools.

One alternative was proposed in what were called "federated" library districts. These would retain autonomous local libraries, but bring them together by means of cooperation and coordination of collections, centralized processing, interlibrary loan and universal borrowing privileges. This was seen as an intermediate step toward consolidated units. Interestingly enough, wholesale consolidation did not occur but the intermediate step of dedicated associations did come about in the following years. (See the trend toward what came to be called "systems" in the 1960–70 period).

The National Plan made many other proposals and recommendations: for stronger state library agencies, for statewide planning, for certification of personnel and, for increased state and federal financial aid. Many of these proposals were carried out, including federal aid within a relatively few years, as we will see shortly. The plan had a definite impact as public libraries moved into a second great upsurge in the 1950s and the 1960s (the first surge forward was in the 1920s).

Both the Post-War standards and the National Plan were the brainchild of Carleton B. Joeckel. He combined a vision of the potential role of the public library with a practical planning sense. He could marshal and articulate the ideas of the coplanners he gathered around him. Some people found him too preoccupied with structure, too prone to put nebulous needs into neat boxes, but there is no question that he was a mover and a shaker.

## Advances in Personnel

Previously noted was the rise of innovative librarians who designed and installed reference, reader's advisory, and children's service in the early decades of the century. These programs spread in the successive years and became standard by midcentury. In libraries of medium and larger size, positions were established which required varied book background and judgment in application—that is, professional positions. Who were the staff members who carried forward with the work and staffed the increasing number of positions?

The number of nationally accredited library school programs increased even during the depression and again after the war;

there were thirty-four such centers by 1950 and, sixty by 1970. Most were at the graduate level and called for a general undergraduate program of study for admission, thus following the recommendation of the Williamson report of 1923. While some effort was made to introduce a preprofessional sequence within the undergraduate years, this did not catch on in the field of librarianship, as it had in the legal and medical fields. Most enrollees in library schools came with a liberal arts background and standard majors in literature, history, and the social sciences. Library study has been and continues to be a kind of specialization in generalization.

Professional graduate training concentrated on functions of libraries: cataloging and classification, book selection, reference-information service, and educational work with adults and children. There was relatively little theory in the curricula, whether of philosophy, organization of knowledge, educational psychology, communications, or reading and readership. Nor was internship built in, as in other professions such as teaching and medicine.

By no means did all occupants of professional positions hold graduate library degrees at midcentury. The Public Library inquiry found that 58 percent in their sample group had undergraduate degrees and only 40 percent had graduate library training.[33] The newer recruits did come from library schools so that the percentages were improving. And there was a definite demand for the library school graduates—actually there was a shortage of qualified candidates some years, not that the rewards of library professional positions were so great in the 1950s. Salaries for librarians not in administrative posts ranged from $2,500 annually on appointment to not much more than $5,000 some years later, this at a time when typical salaries for tenured college professors were in the $10,000–$12,000 range. Nor were librarians held in very great esteem, whether by the general public or by government officials who held the purse strings.

What then attracted promising recruits to the profession? The answer was personal, growing out of their values and career ambitions. They were attracted by the opportunity to serve people and to do so in an intellectual setting and by the challenge of controlling the flood of publications and information in a proliferating society. When questioned, most librarians, then and now, express satisfaction with their choice of vocation. These personal reactions mean that libraries have an extra human resource in motivated staff members with positive attitudes.

By midcentury librarians sought recognition as a profession. Certainly they had some of the attributes: an extensive period of education, certification in some states, and an active national professional association. But public recognition was slow in coming. Why? For one reason because people in general did not readily discern the intellectual discipline of librarianship. The doctor studied medicine, the lawyer studied the law, and the teacher studied the educational process. What body of principles did the librarian study, other than the day-to-day operation of the library? For another reason the public noted that many librarians on the job, for all their knowledge of resources and the useful help they provided, shifted over and engaged in clerical work for periods, like filing, typing, stamping out books, and straightening out shelves. Finally, the salary scale for librarians fell below that of many other professionals, unless the librarian left a service job and took on administration—as though the doctor had to become administrator of a hospital to get adequate remuneration, or the professor, the president of a college.

Various steps were taken to promote professionalism in librarianship—specifically classification of positions, certification, accreditation, staff associations, and even unionization.

Position classification came into place after the war in business and government offices, and was adopted by libraries. Each job was set up to deal with a closely related group of duties, educational requirements were set for each group of positions, salaries were then established for each group, and the groups were put into a sequence to open a career succession. Thus the workforce was organized, suitable recruits could be attracted, and staff groups could work to supplement and reinforce each other.

In libraries this started with separating the professional from nonprofessional or clerical positions. Education considered professional was required for the former. Usually a two-step sequence was arranged for the professional jobs, often called junior and senior librarian. Unfortunately this established a relatively low ceiling for the professionals, which in turn meant a relatively low cap on salary unless the individual moved into an administrative post. Only recently was a third level considered—a specialist librarian, who handles computerized databases and the

Internet—and this has seldom been adopted. However, position classification must be given credit for opening a distinct career sequence for librarians by the 1960s.

Certification by state bodies had spread by the middle of the century, applying to doctors and architects, to accountants and teachers, and to many between. Individuals in such fields were not considered professional unless they had a license. The concept was applied to librarians by a minority of states—fourteen by 1950 and, twenty-one states by 1965, when the movement practically stopped.[34] A typical state regulation read as in this example from New Jersey.

> the body having charge may require that any person hereafter employed in any professional office or position shall hold a professional library certificate. {The certificate shall be issued to} a graduate from a library school accredited by the State Board of Education.[35]

Note that the regulation is permissive and may or may not be adopted by a local library board, and that qualifications are set by the individual state rather than at some national standard. Further, in New Jersey as elsewhere, professional certification does not apply to libraries serving less than five thousand people. All of this is separate from certification for school librarians, which was widespread and included in regulations for teachers.

Certification for public libraries did not spread widely through the states, and it was not adopted by many public libraries. It did not add much to the professional structure for library service.

A different record and conclusion can be applied to accreditation of library schools by the American Library Association. This group organized the Board of Education for Librarianship in 1924. The board set up standards for evaluation, visited schools, and designated those to receive approval. Over the years the ALA revised its standards and its methods of appraisal and maintained a roster of accredited library training centers, the most recent revision being the 1992 *Standards for Accreditation of Master's Programs in Library and Information Studies*. This procedure was widely accepted and became the measure of determining professional status. The effectiveness of accreditation depended upon acceptance by library boards of graduation from an approved school program as the basis of judging professional recruits and many libraries agreed to this. Typically advertisements for personnel specified training in an accredited center. This was a definite contribution to the establishment of a library profession. Note that most of these steps toward professionalization came from within and were not ordained by legislators and the general public as in other professions.

A very different kind of organization—local staff associations in individual libraries—had some effect on the march toward professionalization, although the effect must be judged as marginal. Alice Bryan found staff associations in almost half of the libraries in her study sample for the Public Library Inquiry.[36] Some had been sponsored by management but most were the result of organizing efforts by staff members themselves. Just about one-quarter of the activities of these groups classified as "aiding professional development of staff." The greater effort was in social activities which may well have aided morale but could hardly be attributed to professional enhancement. The second most frequent activity was "working toward improved economic welfare of staff." This could have some relation to professionalization to the extent that it gained improved salaries.

Another factor in the search for professional status was unionization of library staff members, although once again not a major factor. At first glance unionization may be seen as antithetical to professionalization, because of the general conception of unions as an organization for laborers and because of the antipathy of professionals, which is evident among librarians as well as other well-educated vocational groups. However, unions in libraries did engage in some activities that contributed to the status of the members. Besides efforts to improve salaries and working conditions, some of the groups participated in policy making and program planning and helped resolve censorship debates. While membership was greater among nonprofessionals, some established librarians did join the groups.

The most thorough study of unionization in libraries records twenty-nine such organized groups in public libraries in 1975.[37] Most were in larger libraries, some had as much as one-quarter of local staff as members, and almost all were affiliated with national labor organizations. One conclusion of this study is as follows: "The function of group action, or unionization, is to enhance the professional status of the job so it is in accord with the group's desired status as professionals."[38] Certainly no major impact on the status of librarians can be attributed to unions, but such organization was one effort of aspiring professionals.

Thus, some advancement in quality and status of library personnel was made in the middle years, but not much. The content of library education remained technical, which some years later would actually lead to universities closing some library schools. Administrators did seek to separate professional and clerical duties, so that the highly trained staff member did not engage as much in routine tasks. But salaries remained below other fields. Libraries did not extend the "professional" librarian to some librarian specialist category with better compensation. The conclusion of the Public Library Inquiry was probably justified: Librarians are "not a clearly defined professional group."[39]

In the same period, experiments were tried with an intermediate class of positions, between professional and clerical, and usually called subprofessional. Some community colleges offered courses at a beginning technical level. However, this did not really catch on. A good source for subprofessionals was simply the clerical workers already on the job, who could be trained on the job to handle more technical tasks, and who in the process gained a career sequence within the library.

It would be unjustified to say that libriarians did not gain in stature in the middle years. To some degree importance was attached to the duties of the librarian—i.e., the evaluation of publications, organization of materials, and the guidance of individuals in their search for knowledge. The field continued to attract recruits, to the point where there was an oversupply of library-school graduates by 1970 and jobs were not easy to find. The underlying strength of the institution attracted workers of quality and dedication.

The majority of professional recruits have been women. Since 1920 the proportion of female librarians has been 75 to 80 percent. This led to what has been termed "feminization" of the profession, and dire consequences have been attributed to this fact:

> The prevalence of women in the library worked to stunt the process of professionalization, served to maintain the low status accorded to women in matters of the intellect, and helped to perpetuate the public library's marginal position as a cultural institution.[40]

A sweeping indictment of this type prompts one to wonder about the value system of the accuser. Perhaps the answer is in the same article where the author asserts that " the U.S. political and economic system was in basic ways monumentally and monstrously wrong."[41]

Another commentator coined the phrase the "disadvantaged majority."[42] Still another declared, with considerable accuracy so far as it applied to larger libraries, that "80 percent of librarians are women but 90 percent of library administrators are men."[43] No doubt the prominence of women in the library ranks has drawn negative comments from time to time, both from individuals within the ranks as well as from outside, as views have changed about women in business and the professions and as the call for equal opportunity has been voiced. But putting the controversy aside, there can be little question that it is the female staff that has helped to carry the public library on to a place among the approved institutions in society.

Positive signs can be found, starting in the American Library Association itself. A majority of the recent presidents of the association have been women, 70 percent of the members of the council, the legislative body of the group, are of the feminine gender, and the last three Executive Directors before the present incumbent have been women. Slowly the tide turns and balance is gained. What women have done for library service should be a cause for celebration and not an excuse for discrimination.

## Building Collections

The collection is the heart of the matter. This is the means that the library uses to achieve its objectives and this is the resource which the users seek. The collection is built for its community, and theoretically takes on the same contours and characteristics of the community itself.

If the public library existed solely to provide current publications that come into the public eye, there would soon be voices raised as to why we need the library at all. Readers of the current output could simply go to a bookstore and purchase the items they desired, and at a cost no greater than they already pay through taxes to maintain the library. It is the collection that is the unique resource, waiting to supply the particular title needed, available for studying a topic that may have no relation to current publication. The library is not a convenience store; it is a supermarket.

Building the collection is not easy. Here is a book on the early stages of the Russian Revolution; local people have displayed little interest in this period, so it can be passed over. Here is a biography of Cleopatra; perhaps thanks to Elizabeth Taylor there is interest in this early figure, so we will acquire. Now a book—a whole book—devoted to the cooking of prunes; we have a strong collection on cooking, including several publications with sections on prunes, so this will be rejected. And a volume on the baseball scandal of the 1920s appears; sports always get a response, so an order will be placed for this title. The examination goes on through literally thousands of items.

This is selection in the narrow sense, proceeding item by item. Over the years there has developed a concept of collection development, building resources from a foundation of principles. This starts with clarification of mission of the individual library, proceeds to a body of articulated objectives shared by all those who engage in selection, rests on a clear and updated analysis of the community served, leading to a formal statement of selection criteria, and involving possible actual physical examination of the publication under consideration and/or a systematic and critical examination of reviewing media. The librarian has help in the opinions of others, but in the end the decision is his or hers alone.

So the judgment calls are made, whether each item in isolation, or with the guidance of clear objectives. In smaller libraries one staff member may make most of the decisions, while in larger libraries many individuals participate, each with his or her own interests and values. Sometimes the actual books are in hand to examine under the Greenaway plan, but often the selector must work from reviews, which may be delayed for more specialized books. In the early decades of the century copies of the books were seldom in hand.

Item by item the collections are built up, the selectors on the one hand holding a general impression of the purposes of the library in mind, and on the other hand having a general impression of community and users. It is more an art than a science. In time the result stands on shelf after shelf; the die is cast, the core collection established.

The first reaction the objective observer has to the standing collection is that most of the books stay on the shelves, waiting for users. The Public Library Inquiry was to find at midcentury that 10 percent of the collection accounts for 90 percent of the use. In all but the largest subject-department agencies, the heavier use is in the fiction section. The nonfiction collection is more a wholesale stock waiting for occasional retail use. Seldom do libraries systematically check to identify "deadwood."

Constantly present in the building of collections is the question of demand versus quality. The arguments on both sides will continue through the century and appear again in a comprehensive publication on public-library administration appearing in the last decade.[44]

The question appeared near the beginning, at the founding of the Boston Public Library in the 1850s. Edward Everett, one of the trustees, stressed the cultured person who should have the "means of education" within reach.[45] On the other side was George Ticknor, another trustee: ". . . the pleasant literature of the day should be available to the whole people at the only time when they care for it, i.e., when it is fresh and new."[46] Thus the division was formed between serving educational or popular interests.

Those who favor "demand" as the criterion for building the collection rest their case on the fact that many readers request bestsellers, light romances, and mysteries, and it is the people who pay for the library with their taxes. Any other policy would be antidemocratic and elitist, according to this view. Further, those who accept the more ephemeral literature would point out that recreation—pure diversion—is of social value in its own right; the stress is on re-creation. Moreover, it is asserted that reading of this material can lead, by close physical association, to examination and possible consumption of more substantial publications, although there is little evidence in support of this point. Whether they formally subscribe to this position or not, most public libraries provide popular provisional literature and often in multiple copies; demand is recognized.

Those who argue for the "quality" criterion cite the underlying educational purpose of the agency. What money is available should be put into substantial publications in support of this purpose, and librarians should not be tempted by material that will be passe and stand unused in a few years. This side pushes its case by claiming that providing popular literature of the day makes the public library no more than a free bookstore. Government provides money, according to this view, not to save the cost of $10 or $20 for a novel for the local resident, but to build a unique educational resource.

Most libraries find a middle ground. They supply the new book by Gene Stratton Porter (1920s) and Danielle Steel (1990s) and at the same time they stock the history output of Winston Churchill (1920s) and Thurow's *Future of Capitalism* (1990s). They live with whatever contradiction is involved in these policies and are not disposed to search their souls. This leads to accumulations of the literature of yesteryear which libraries discard from time to time and to additions to the educational shelves which many people see as the reason for being of the agency. What this duality of purpose will do to the public library in the Information Age is yet to be determined.

Some reconciliation of the problem can be gained when a library takes time out to put together a mission statement and to clarify its purposes and objectives. Involving the staff and trustees in this process tends to bring issues to the surface and helps to reach agreement on goals. If the role of the agency in the Digital Age, and particularly its function as an information source, is put into the consideration, a general direction and strategy for the future may emerge.

On this ground selectors find their way among the various selection aids. First come the prepublication announcements in *Publishers Weekly* and the *Kirkus Reviews*. Local newspapers have reviews, as do *New York Times*, and the news weeklies. *Library Journal* has briefer reviews written usually by librarians, which come closer to the decisions the selectors must make, and the same holds true of the listings in the semimonthly *Booklist* of the American Library Association. If enough reviews are done, they will be excerpted in the *Book Review Digest*. The more thorough evaluations come out later in subject and technical journals. Librarians use these sources like a skilled worker uses the tools on a workbench.

Then there are the retrospective aids to help start a collection or to check back on present holdings. Examples are the longstanding *Standard Catalog for Public Libraries* (now *Public Library*

*Catalog*) of the H. W. Wilson Co., and the recent Bowker *Best Books for Public Libraries* (1992). There is a contradiction here. On the one hand is the principle that all libraries are different, with their own purposes and unique community of users, and on the other are these retrospective aids with their standard listings. "Which are the best books" for which public libraries? The best explanation is that librarians assume that there is a core collection that fits all agencies with special publications added around the core to meet the needs of local constituencies. This is not consistent with the theory, but it may reflect reality; most public libraries have many of the same titles even though their communities are not the same.

In considering current publications, libraries reject many of the titles printed, thus opening themselves to the charge of censorship, for readers are denied access to the rejected items. Censorship is rejection on the grounds of objectionable content, material with which the librarian does not agree or that has been challenged by individuals or groups in the community. On the other hand, evaluation of a book on the basis of the clarity and thoroughness of its presentation is not censorship. Not all publications can be purchased with the budget available, so criteria of quality must be exercised. By and large librarians have been respected and supported for their judgments, but some instances of personal or group prejudice have occurred in the professional ranks. And the issue is not all in the past; it appears again concerning pornographic and other content on the Internet. Will the library provide access to material on the computer that they would not place in book form on the shelves? The librarian acts as a filter, a filter we trust, without holes of prejudice. In any case, the volumes accumulate on the shelves, the collection gets larger and larger. As time goes by more and more of the holdings stand unused. In fact, libraries claim that they have run out of shelf space and need an addition or a new building, even while the unused items remain. We have accumulated literally millions of books that will never be opened.

This leads to the other side of the coin, deselecting or discarding of items from the collection. Librarians use the term "weeding" for this operation, and it is appropriate: material past bloom is removed to allow remaining plants to flourish. Unless this is done, the collection becomes outdated and it becomes harder to find what one wants. The aim is to weed out books least likely to be used. Again judgment is called for. If selection principles are uncertain, those for weeding are even more so. One hesitates to remove an item that might be called for next week or even next year.

But with interlibrary loan well developed, and now with systems and networks in place (see the 1960–79 section), weeding should be more vigorous than is usually practiced. In the past the usual procedure, for deciding whether to discard an infrequently used book, was to retain the title because there might be a call for it. Now it should more frequently be removed because the interlibrary loan and system apparatus are readily at hand. Librarians have built these cooperative systems and fallback procedures and make good use of them, but do not seem to have confidence in them when it comes to deselecting and cutting collections.

How to identify publications to be discarded? Some calls are self-evident. Where information is clearly outdated—as in health and technology—or where duplicates stand on the shelves after demand has decreased, the decision can be made without hesitation. Beyond that, evidence of infrequent use—say no circulation in one year or two years—can be used. The catch here is that current technical methods for charging and discharging do not readily provide this information, for cards within books are seldom used. Spinemarking can be employed in this case,[47] but it is a slow and elaborate process. However done, a rule of thumb has been that close to 5 percent of public-library collections should be retired each year, and this figure is probably too small.

We have remarked before that librarians are hesitant to acquire hard evidence about use and users, preferring to depend on general impressions. One would think that the administrator would want to know just what is used, not solely for weeding purposes but also for collection building purposes. But analysis of circulation is seldom attempted. A few libraries do try to determine what publications are used within the building by asking readers not to reshelve their books, but this also is uncommon.

Despite this hesitation to analyze, by and large the selections and collections that librarians have built are generally accepted without criticism by users. Of course few people have any standard by which to judge. They are grateful for what they can get and do not often ask for more; if what they seek is not provided, they leave quietly—and may not return.

Yet thousands of collections exist across the land, providing entrance to the recorded world of knowledge and to wholesome entertainment to most residents. This is a resource of incalculable value. The country is the better for having this treasure, whether it is perfectly adjusted to the community or not, whether it contains deadwood or not.

## State Library Agencies

State library agencies are the missing link in our story thus far. In many cases they provided important services—in some cases actual leadership in the development of statewide plans and programs. Yet most had a slow and sporadic growth between 1900 and 1950, by which time they were ready to assume their full role.

There were exceptions. James L. Gillis, State Librarian in California, divided his agency in 1900 into three parts, a historical department, a Department of Legislative Reference and Statistics, and a Department of Public Libraries, thus recognizing responsibility for collection building, for legislative service, and for promoting libraries over the state. The work of the last of these units resulted in a base of county libraries in California, which early on gave local service an organization and strength that was distinctive in the country, until the tax revolt there in the 1970s and after. At the turn of the century, Melvil Dewey, with his innovative mind and energy, put New York State into the vanguard. His library school had moved from Columbia University by that time, and he was not only head of the school but also State Librarian and Secretary of the Board of Regents of the University of the State of New York. He laid the foundation for a strong collection in Albany, with special sections on medicine, education, children's literature, and even a "Women's Library." He also shipped collections of one hundred books around to small towns in the state, thus planting the seed for formation of local public libraries.

But in most states a long period of organization and reorganization was to ensue. Some state libraries resisted the concept of extension and separate state library commissions had to be formed for the purpose. In some instances state library agencies were incorporated into state departments of education—after all, the argument made for state action on libraries was that they were part of the educational program, which was a state responsibility. So organized, some state library agencies languished as fringe parts of large departments, although this was not universally true—witness the rapid growth of the State Library in the New York State Education Department. Wherever located, state library agencies sometimes found themselves competing against each other for the same parcel of money. It took decades for these problems to sort themselves out.

By 1950—fortunately in time for the 1956 Library Services Act of the federal government which provided grants to the states—the reorganizations had pretty well settled down. At present nineteen states operate under state library boards or commissions. Seventeen are within state departments of education and the remaining fourteen have varying structures, including three (Florida, Illinois, and Tennessee) which are part of secretary of state offices.[48] Unusual arrangements were made in Maryland, where the state contracted with the Enoch Pratt Free Library in Baltimore to serve as the state-level collection, and in Hawaii where one system provides both state-level and local service, including public libraries.

The state agencies moved step by step into providing and promoting direct service to residents lacking local facilities. In some instances loans of packages of books were made for extended periods (six months or a year) to local organizations or individuals, who in turn opened them to nearby residents. Book wagons were put on the roads, and by the 1920s and 1930s mobile units which went to unserved districts. Now we had not just an agency of last resort in the state capital, through interlibrary loan, but also an agency of first resort within localities, in the form of a state-operated bookmobile. At the same time promotional efforts were made to encourage unserved localities to establish their own public libraries, and with considerable success as the public-library movement spread.

Once smaller libraries were established, the state agencies advised and counseled them, and beyond that provided collections of visual materials and in some cases processed materials for them (that is, acquired and cataloged new books). As increased state money became available the agencies occasionally went further and helped local units to join OCLC (now the On-line Computer Library Center) and also provided funds to build union catalogs showing the holdings of a group of libraries. By the 1950s the state and localities were genuinely working together to improve facilities for all residents.

Then the federal government joined the team with provision of federal money, first in 1956 (the Library Services Act) and then more in 1964 (the Library Services and Construction Act). The earlier legislation concentrated on rural areas, and soon two hundred bookmobiles were traveling the back roads. The later legislation extended money to all sizes and levels and gave a shot in the arm to much-needed construction. A few states managed to use part of the federal money to reduce their own appropriations, but almost universally the federal dollars went for the purposes for which they were provided.

Perhaps the most important function taken on by the state level was that of planning for and carrying out a statewide system of library service. Many of the state agencies can properly be called the leader in promoting the development of statewide public-library organization in the decades since the 1950s. Having helped establish the local foundation, the states then sought to pull localities together into a superstructure. Federal money was used for this purpose, and federal policies furthered the cause by emphasizing the need for planning. (Examples of the results can be found in the discussion of "Systems and Networks" in the 1960–79 section of this history).

Among the unsung movers and shakers who built up library facilities throughout the century, and particularly in the last half, should be added the state librarians and library commission heads. Many of them, because of their statewide view, thought in wider terms than the administrators of individual local units, and they had a positive effect. Having brought local libraries into existence, they then proceeded to fit them together in systems and networks. In substance they mobilized resources within their states to gain the greatest joint return for all. We certainly do not have a unified and coordinated national program of public library service, giving equal service to every citizen, but we do have such programs within some states.

The State of Washington has gone a step further. The Washington Library Network (WLN) seeks to coordinate resources on the West Coast and indeed on around the Pacific Rim. Other regions have made efforts to bring together groups of states, using state agencies for the purpose. Coordination into regional groups is one possible development for the future.

Besides responsibilities for extension and for coordination throughout the commonwealth, state libraries also took on other jobs such as provision of materials for the blind and the handicapped, for government documents, and for historical collections. In these respects the state agencies were acting as public libraries, providing resources directly to users; they should be added to the roster of publicly supported units open to all residents, which was the definition of the public library with which we started in the beginning.

As in the case of the multiple purposes which we noted early on for local public libraries, now we have a parallel situation at the state level, with agencies adding to their purposes and programs without always having the resources to carry out their aspirations. The wide range of responsibilities is reflected in the *Standards for Library Functions at the State Level* adopted by the American Library Association in 1963.

All this leads to the question of how well supported the state agencies are to carry out their multiple responsibilities. Do they have the means to carry the present load and to meet the new challenges of the Information Age? Certainly the state-provided financial aid varies widely, from under ten cents per capita in Florida to $3 per capita in Alaska and $4 in New York.[49] Two surveys later in the century raised concerns about the adequacy of funding at the state level. Moneypenny raised questions in this regard and commented on the library functions being at the edge of power politics.[50] Summers expressed his concerns almost twenty years later.[51] Both also noted a limited or lukewarm support for state library agencies on the part of the library world—public, academic, and special.

State library agencies in substance completed the movement for local public libraries in the first half of the century and then were lead players in coordinating the many units to work together in the second half of the century. Will they again be out front in the next years as the public library seeks to find its place in the world of digital communication?

Federal money enabled state library agencies to have their full impact. Now in the last decade of the century the federal government is pulling back from activities that can be passed to the state level. (The era of big government is over.) And many of the state governments are in turn cutting back on their financial commitments. It is a moot point whether state library agencies can continue to be out front on their own.

## Notes

1. Robert D. Leigh, *The Public Library in the United States.* (New York: Columbia University Press, 1950), 3
2. Bernard Berelson, *The Library's Public.* Alice I. Byran, *The Public Librarian.* Oliver Garceau, *The Public Library in the Political Process.* James L. McCamy, *Government Publications for the Citizen.* William Miller, *The Book Industry.* Gloria Waldron, *The Information Film.* All published by the Columbia University Press.
3. Robert D. Leigh, *The Public Library*, 51.
4. Ibid, 74.
5. Ibid, 99.
6. Ibid, 107.
7. Ibid, 96.
8. Bernard Berelson, *The Library's Public.* (New York: Columbia University Press, 1949)
9. Ibid, 127.
10. Ibid, 18.
11. Eliza A. Gleason, *The Southern Negro and the Public Library.* (Chicago: University of Chicago Press, 1941), 184
12. Ibid, 185.
13. A. P. Marshall, "Service to Afro-Americans," in Sidney L. Jackson, ed. *A Century of Service.* (Chicago: American Library Association, 1976), 68.
14. *Access to Public Libraries: A Research Project* (Chicago: American Library Association, 1963).
15. Ibid, 59.
16. E. J. Josey, "Libraries, Reading and the Liberation of Black People." *Library Scene*, vol. 1 (1972), 4.
17. U.S. Bureau of Labor Statistics, *Library Manpower: A Study of Demand and Supply,* Bulletin 1852. (Washington, D.C.: Government Printing Office, 1975), 25.
18. *American Libraries,* vol. 27 no. 2 (1996), 7.

19. Edward G. Holley, *The Library Services and Construction Act.* (Greenwich, Conn.: JAI Press, 1983), 56–57.

20. Doris R. Wats and Elaine Simpson, "Students in the Public Library." *Wilson Library Bulletin,* vol. 37 (1962), 242–57.

21. Oliver Garceau, *The Public Library in the Political Process* (New York: Columbia University Press, 1949), 239.

22. E. J. Josey, *Politics and the Support of Libraries.* (New York: Neal-Schuman, 1990).

23. Cynthia Jenkins, Ibid, 45.

24. *Fact Book,* Division of Library Development, New York State Library; 3.

25. E. J. Josey, Politics, 134–43.

26. *New York Times.* 6 December, 1995, A23

27. Carleton B. Joeckel and Amy Winslow, *A National Plan for Public Library Service.* (Chicago: American Library Association, 1948).

28. Committee on Post-War Planning, *Post-War Standards for Public Libraries.* (Chicago: American Library Association, 1943).

29. Ibid, 21.

30. Ibid, 76.

31. Ibid, 62.

32. Carleton B. Joeckel, *National Plan.*

33. Robert D. Leigh, *Public Library,* 194.

34. Alice I. Bryan, *Public Librarian,* 320.

35. Alex Ladenson, *American Library Laws.* (Chicago: American Library Association, 1983), 1271.

36. Alice I. Bryan, *Public Librarian,* 264.

37. Theodore L. Guyton, *Unionization; the Viewpoint of Librarians.* (Chicago: American Library Association, 1975).

38. Ibid, 173.

39. Alice I. Bryan, *Public Librarian,* 431.

40. Dee Garrison, "Women in Librarianship," in Sidney L. Jackson, ed. *A Century of Service.* (Chicago: American Library Association, 1976), 146.

41. Ibid, 163.

42. Anita Schiller, "The Disadvantaged Majority: Women Employees in Libraries." *American Libraries,* vol. 1 (1970), 345.

43. Wendy De Fichy, "Affirmative Action: Equal Opportunity for Women in Library Management." *College and Research Libraries,* vol. 34 (1973), 1951.

44. Alice Gertzog and Edwin Beckerman, *Administration of the Public Library.* (Metuchen, N.J.: Scarecrow Press, 1994), 170–74.

45. Jesse Shera, *Foundations of the Public Library.* (Chicago: University of Chicago, 1949), 218.

46. Ibid, 219.

47. Stanley J. Slote, *Welding Library Collections*. (Littleton, Colo.: Libraries Unlimited, 1982), 134–42.

48. William G. Asp, "The State of State Library Agencies" in Charles R. McClure, (ed.) *State Library Services and Issues* (Norwood, N.J.: Ablex, 1986), 18.

49. Charles R. McClure, Ibid, 63.

50. Philip Moneypenny, *The Library Functions of the States*. (Chicago: American Library Association, 1966).

51. F. William Summers, *The State Library Agencies: A Survey Project Report*. (Chicago: American Library Association, 1983).

# 6

# Promise and Disillusionment, 1960–1970

President Kennedy came in on the slogan "Get the country moving again." President Johnson followed with the Great Society. Then the United States went to war six thousand miles away. The promise was broken; a profound change occurred in the American spirit.

The wound to the American spirit caused by the Vietnam War is hard to exaggerate. Some young people reacted aggressively, even violently. The picture one remembers is of the young woman kneeling on the street over the body of a student at Kent State University, a student who had been killed by a police bullet. I myself stood holding hands with other professors in a circle around the administration building at Columbia University while students stormed up the steps. Other young people went off to Woodstock, smoked marijuana, let their hair grow long, and burned their brassieres.

John Kennedy brought high hopes to the presidency, even though his social program was vague. He stumbled in the Bay of Pigs affair but stood firm in the Cuban Missile Crisis. Then an assassin's bullet brought Camelot to an end.

Lyndon Johnson, coarse and tough, pushed legislation through Congress for his Great Society—a war on poverty, civil rights,

Medicare, aid to education and libraries. Then, tragically, he got bogged down in Vietnam because he vowed not to be the first president to lose a war, his Great Society faded, and he decided not to run for a second elected term in office.

Richard Nixon, persistent and crafty, finally finished the Vietnam War and opened contact with Communist China. It was the Watergate scandal that pulled him down. When he faced impeachment for tampering with evidence about his own involvement, he resigned from office, the first president in U.S. history to do so.

A peanut farmer from Georgia finished out the 1970s. President Carter arranged a peace settlement in the Near East, got through a Panama Canal Treaty, and tried to obtain an agreement to limit nuclear arms. But he fought with Congress, failed in trying to rescue American hostages taken in Iran, ran into high inflation, and was beaten by Ronald Reagan in 1980. Jimmy Carter has gained more stature since leaving office with his project called Habitat for Humanity and with his diplomacy in international disputes.

All four presidents of the two decades were brought down in defeat by circumstances beyond their control.

Yet these continued to be the years of an "affluent society." You could buy a mink-handled beer opener at B. Altman's in New York City. Two cars stood in many garages, all the new kitchen appliances were bought and in time paid for, designer labeled clothes became the fashion, and houses became larger and larger. Huge shopping malls attracted the customers, easy credit and installment buying lured them on, and advertising told consumers of products they didn't know they wanted.

The American school came under a barrage of criticism during these years. We were told that Johnny can't read and that the nation was at risk. Among the more influential reports were James Conant's *The American High School Today* (1959), Charles Silberman's *Crisis in the Classroom* (1970), and Jonathan Kozol's *Death at an Early Age* (1985). The evidence offered to document shortcomings were falling test scores and anecdotes of graduates unable to perform on the job or to handle college courses.

What was sometimes forgotten in these indictments was that the schools were taking in students from wider segments of the population, some from slum conditions and broken families and some with a native language other than English. While part of the criticism was no doubt deserved, millions of young people were performing well and preparing for careers and further education.

By 1960, 90 percent of American homes had television. Programs in great abundance came over the airwaves. Much of that reflected a mass culture, what some critics called a vulgarization of taste, as program content reached for the lowest common denominator. One might suppose that television might take the pressure off public libraries for providing light diversional reading, but this was not the case.

The more creative literature of these decades was uniformly marked by a pervasive pessimism. Samuel Beckett, turned off by the prevailing trends, has one of his characters say: "I have been a man long enough. I shall not put up with it anymore." Rachel Carson sent a chill through the land with her *Silent Spring*.

Paradoxically, these were years of creativity in the arts. Imaginative architecture appeared in New York City in Lincoln Center and the Guggenheim Museum, and in other cities Mikhail Baryshnikov teamed up with George Balanchine to produce exciting ballets. Progress also occurred in science and technology; in medicine organ transplants and identification of DNA were achieved. In space flight we saw "one small step for man, one giant step for mankind." The Alaska gas pipeline and the Concorde airplane were other advances.

But the net result of these two decades was widespread disillusion. Vietnam and Watergate and poverty could not be put out of mind. The country turned to the future with an impaired spirit.

The women's movement came to the surface in this period. Betty Freidan's *The Feminine Mystique*[1] came out in 1963; the National Organization for Woman (NOW) was formed in 1966 "to take action to bring women into full participation in the mainstream of American society." Now the aim was to eliminate discrimination in employment, job promotion, compensation, government service, even college admission. In public schools, where the preponderance of teachers were women, there were few female superintendents or principals.[2] Reformers directed attention to the female stereotypes in textbooks and disproportionate expenditures in schools for athletic activities for boys. Even language had to be de-sexed.

Congressional hearings were held in 1970 and the Women's Educational Equity Act was passed in 1974. Progress occurred in the 1970s with women appearing in the ranks of engineers, lawyers, doctors, etc. Actually, as we have seen, women had appeared in leadership roles in librarianship many years before, a harbinger that is little recognized.

These were turbulent decades, with war, assassinations and widespread cynicism. However, the public library, for a minority, came to play a role foreseen by few of its advocates, that of a compass to hold the course, to sustain traditional values and protect national hope and confidence. Fed up with the mess? Go to the public library and read Emily Dickinson or James Michener.

## Overview of Library Service, 1960–1979

Despite the malaise of the time, the 1960s and 1970s were positive years for public libraries. A professional staff was in place. Administrators learned to utilize use planning and evaluation. The basic structure was coordinated in systems and networks during these decades. Most significant was the gaining of federal financial aid. And through this time the respect paid libraries as part of a lifelong educational service resulted in reasonable although certainly not bountiful financial support.

The achievement of federal financial aid for libraries was a clear step forward. The goal of many years was realized and the impact on libraries was crystal clear. Service was stimulated, both rural and urban, and construction revived. The federal money in turn gave state library agencies a shot in the arm, and also prompted increased local support in some jurisdictions. The federal money kept the public-library movement alive and vital at a strategic time.

The reorganization of public libraries into joint systems and networks moved forward, an accomplishment of considerable note because it strengthened all libraries along the line and removed the isolation of many small agencies. There has been criticism of the trend to larger systems, on the grounds that it improves resources available from a distance instead of bringing materials directly into the lives of people. In this view the critical point is what stands on the shelves when the reader comes through the door of the local library. Systems of libraries strengthen the resources available to determined readers who are prepared to wait for what they need, but this does not help the bulk of users who turn only to what is on the shelves. Users of a unit in a system gain by having access to resources in other, often larger libraries. But for this to work they must know what is available to them, and some libraries have been less than energetic in educating their patrons about what the plan can do for them.

On the administrative front an element of evaluation of performance and service rendered was injected into practice, an element that had been missing in library management. In some cases this was admittedly more gesture and lip service and did not lead to fundamental change on any broad scale. Somehow librarians have not been motivated to find out how well they are doing.

Renewed efforts to expand the base of use and users produced limited results. Outreach had been tried at intervals over the century, in an effort to broaden the response to public-library service, and this effort continued in the 1960s and 1970s. Public relations and publicity were carried on—at the national level by the American Library Association, in statewide programs, and at the local level—but with sparse evidence of reaching nonusers.

With the increasing split between rich and poor, the problem of inner-city service came more to the fore, but the public library has not proven to be the agency to provide a safety net for low-education areas. The public library remains a mainstream agency, serving a middle level of user groups, both in terms of financial and educational background. If this is the "people's university," less than half of the people are enrolled, and there are few additional applicants.

In this period public libraries ventured further into multimedia provision. They were seeking to go beyond the book and become the agency for all forms of communication. In this section the ventures into the various forms are reviewed. In what can be called near-book material (periodicals, for example) it will be apparent that public libraries have cut out a place and have a regular user group. But in other forms that are also impressions on a page (pamphlets, for example, and pictorial material) libraries have not found their niche. In other forms of communication not related to print (recordings and films, for example) public libraries have gained only a precarious foothold and have been pushed aside by commercial outlets. In the following review of multimedia, it is interesting to see such terms as "supplement" or "adjunct" or even "orphan" appearing to describe the place that the different forms hold in the service program.

A shortage of trained librarians appeared in the 1960s. The economy of the country was robust in these years, so there were many opportunities outside of librarianship open to able young people. On their side, libraries still struggled with the uncertain image of the librarian, and the below-average salary level had been rectified only to a small degree. This was significant because new recruits in the 1960s would become the leaders and administrators of the 1980s and 1990s, when the public library would face the challenge of digitized information and new electronic communication.

Some strains appeared in the much-respected children's program of the public library. School libraries appeared at the elementary level and took over part of the task of stimulating and guiding young readers. Questions were raised as to why the two collections and staffs needed to be maintained. Public libraries shifted more to the preschool years and this trend continued on into the 1980s. Latchkey children turned up more in the libraries; with wives and mothers employed, some youngsters turned to the library for shelter and activity. For all children the matter of open access to adult materials came to the fore; the American Library Association amended its Library Bill of Rights to approve such access, taking the position that it was the responsibility of parents to limit the children's reading.

The number of public libraries in the United States now approached 10,000, with close to 6,000 additional branch units. The agency was well established in the fabric of American life. Internally, the problems it faced were adequacy of financial support, organization and interlibrary relations, and maintenance of an educated and motivated staff. These problems were met to a degree sufficient enough for the public library to serve as a source of continuing values and achievement; a source much needed by a restless and disillusioned public.

## Federal Financial Aid to Libraries

Financial support of the public library came originally from the locality—town, city, or county. This was the case for the predecessors of the agency in the nineteenth century, when local individuals and groups put up the necessary money. And the pattern continued when local governments authorized libraries to be open to all residents and provided financial support. The taproot for the institution is the locality.

After World War II the state level of government became more involved in promoting library service and in some cases was drawn into providing some financial aid, first for extending facilities to rural areas and then for general improvement of service. The strongest argument for such action was that education was a responsibility of the state and the public library came to be seen as part of the educational system.

The American Library Association began soliciting federal aid in the 1920s, but it was to be a long, uphill battle. Various stumbling blocks stood in the way. Education was seen as a state responsibility—why should the federal government be involved? School aid stumbled on the issue of public and parochial schools—would money go to both? And what of race relations—would money go to segregated facilities? Library representatives had to talk out these issues with members of Congress and their staff groups.

The ALA established a Washington Office in 1945. First Julia Bennett, and later Germaine Krettek, handled the office and they are given credit for shepherding library legislation through to passage. They had first to learn the reality of national politics. Librarians and ALA officers made frequent trips to Washington to testify before Congressional committees.

A decision was made early to proceed separately from school interests, in order to avoid the religious issue. Also it was decided to focus first on rural service, to reach the unserved villages and farms of the country. This was a tangible problem for which sympathy could be aroused. It was stressed that 27 million people lacked any access to books and reference sources.

The bookmobile was used effectively in the campaign. This was to be the primary means for getting out into the countryside. Different bookmobiles were brought in to Washington from time to time and parked in the congressional parking lot. Members of Congress had their picture taken in front of the machine if it was from their district, and other members stopped by out of curiosity. The story was passed around of the farm wife who visited the bookmobile in the farmyard and then called her husband: "Hiram, come here quick. We're rich, we're rich!"[3]

In 1950 a Public Library Service Demonstration Bill was introduced by Senators Lester Hill (Alabama) and George Aiken (Vermont) and by Congresswoman Emily Taft Douglas (Illinois) in the House. The two senators would prove to be strong proponents in the years ahead (Congresswoman Douglas was shortly defeated). The bill passed in the Senate but was defeated in the House, 161 to 164—a distinct setback.

But lobbying continued. The Library Services Act was introduced in 1951 by Senators Hill and Aiken and Paul Douglas and by eight representatives in the House. Once again it was an uphill fight, but the bill finally passed both houses by 1956 and was signed by president Eisenhower.

The Library Services Act was aimed directly at rural service. It called for state control of funds, and states were to submit plans to the U.S. Office of Education for approval. The legislation specified $7.5 million per year, but only $2 million was appropriated in 1957, $5 million by 1958, $6 million by 1959 and the full amount by 1960 and 1961.

Then the proponents sought a five-year extension. This was not easy to achieve, for librarians had originally asserted that only a five-year demonstration was needed. They ran into the congressional view that there was nothing more permanent than a temporary agency.

Now the presidents got into the act. President Kennedy's budget request for 1963 specified "improvement of community library services for people of all ages" and concluded that "all public libraries will be eligible for Federal assistance, including construction."[4] President Johnson followed suit in his State of the Union address in 1964: "Let this session be known as the session that helped to build more schools, more libraries, and more hospitals than any single session in the history of our Republic."[5]

The Library Services and Construction Act passed in early 1964 (89 to 7 in the Senate, 254 to 107 in the House). An extension to the Act in 1966 passed the House by a vote of 336 to 2. The cause of libraries had come a long way at the federal level.

The new provisions achieved the following:

- population limit of ten thousand removed, aid now applied to all libraries;
- construction included, just when the Carnegie buildings were falling into disuse;

- strengthening of state library agencies;
- and interlibrary cooperation to be encouraged, just when the concept of systems came to the fore.

A total of $73 million was authorized for these several purposes.[6]

It had been a long and skillful campaign. The first stumbling block was the belief that libraries were a state and local responsibility, and therefore the federal government had no role to play. The promoters got around this by stressing rural service, which had been missed by both the states and the localities. Members of Congress felt that they were helping the farmers in their districts, a heartwarming purpose that obscured the federal state debate. Also, the legislation wisely placed administration of the grants according to plans prepared by each of the states, not by prescriptions from Washington.

Once they had some supporters in Congress, the library proponents were able to educate this core on the returns that would accrue if financial aid was extended to urban as well as rural areas, and beyond service to construction, and in time even to joint and cooperative efforts to improve service—note the 336 to 2 vote in the House in 1966. All along the way was the basic appeal of library service—who could be against providing books for people? As president Johnson put it:

> Those who do not read are not much better off than those who cannot read . . . As the boundaries of learning are pushed back, our need for the storehouse of knowledge grows greater.[7]

The timing for federal aid for libraries was right. The Library Services and Construction Act was part of the Great Society movement of the 1960s. Earlier it was difficult to drum up support of federal aid to education. Later it would run into the antigovernment philosophy of the Nixon and Reagan years.

A few years later (1970) the National Commission on Libraries and Information Science (NCLIS) was created, with membership to be composed of citizens and experts from mostly outside the ranks of librarians. Its task was to "point toward an effective and efficient library system for the future."[8] Several dedicated and distinguished individuals have served on the commission over the years. NCLIS has been a presence but not a force in library affairs and in federal financial aid. The agency has seldom exerted influence in the inner circles of government planning. Most of the initiative and planning have come from the American Library Association.

The LSCA had a discernible effect on library programs across the country. The state agencies were energized. Many local libraries took advantage of the federal money. New Jersey, for example, reported a doubling of circulation.[9] The federal grants had a stimulating effect on local financial effort, so that one dollar of LSCA money would lead to several dollars of additional appropriations. A city would propose a million-dollar building, receive $100,000 of federal help through the state, and somehow find the rest of the funds. This success was evident during the 1960s and into the 1970s.

However, back in Washington progress leveled off; several of the strongest supporters of federal aid fell by the wayside. As a result of the Vietnam debate, President Johnson decided not to run again. Senator Hill retired in 1968. Representative John Fogarty, a bricklayer from Rhode Island and a strong voice for libraries in the House, died suddenly of a heart attack in 1967. Federal aid continued but was not expanded.

President Nixon favored zero funding for libraries but was overruled by a Congress supportive of libraries. He then resorted to "impoundment"—holding up funds even though they had been appropriated — but did not succeed with library money. This led to a headline in the newspaper *Portland Oregonian* reading: "Would You Like for President Nixon to be Your Librarian?" The Washington office of the American Library Association, which had fought so hard for the LSCA legislation, now found itself in a rearguard action to protect what had been gained. Fortunately libraries had many friends in Congress. And editorials in papers across the country and in periodicals such as the *Saturday Review* supported the cause. The favorable public opinion in regard to libraries, which we noted throughout this history, is still one of the strongest assets of the public library.

The rearguard action continued through the Reagan years and on into the 1990s. Then, late in the century, the Congress passed the Library Services and Technology Act, to take effect in 1998. The Clinton years lack the commitment of a Kennedy or Johnson. President Clinton has held the line but has not markedly increased federal aid for libraries, despite the claim by the administration that the agency has a key role to play in the Digital Age.

## Systems and Networks

Over the years the problem of inadequate library government units has been cited frequently in this history. Public libraries sprouted like plants in a field over the first half of the century, a few large and substantial, more of medium size, and many very small and circumscribed. Most public libraries by 1960 were simply too small and limited to have any chance of rendering a reasonable level of service.

The National Plan (1948) actually proposed combining and reducing the number of library districts from 6,000 to 2,000,[10] in order to have a decidedly smaller number of units covering the country and with stronger resources in each; branch libraries would bring facilities close to people. The Public Library inquiry (1950) stressed the same theme.[11] Statewide surveys in Pennsylvania, Missouri, New Jersey, and New Hampshire also wrestled with the same problem. The matter became even more pressing with suburban growth around big cities in the 1950s and 1960s, for this brought additional units into existence.

Actually "larger units" of service had appeared much earlier in the state of California, which emphasized the county as the governmental base for library service. California counties on the average are much larger than in other states. Also, the concept there was of a unified administrative unit, which meant that separate libraries would have to give up their identity to join the countywide facility. Sound county libraries were established in California and also some lesser county units in other states, but this form did not spread across the country. It was not the solution to the problem of existing small and limited libraries.

Nor did the sweeping reorganization envisioned in the National Plan come into existence. Public libraries were too much local creatures, with roots deep in the structure of local communities. Established libraries, whether in smaller towns or in suburbs, were not inclined to join with larger county units or with central cities. Each separate agency built up its own affiliated adherents, made up of established boards of directors and established staffs, backed up in many instances by local government officials and community groups. A unified larger district would not come into existence unless these various adherents agreed to the shift. They did not want to give up their own local library nor did they want to become enmeshed in the mounting problems of central cities.

The logjam was broken by the concept of systems. "Systems" here refers not to existing unified libraries—such as the Chicago Public Library system—but to multijurisdictional entities relating two or more libraries into a common program. The essential element in this idea was that separate libraries would not give up their identity or authority but would work together within larger coordinating units in which they would be voluntary members. Still with their separate identities, they would derive benefits from the combined strength of the group while themselves contributing to that strength.

The concept, on the face of it, did not look very promising. It required each library to work with others (didn't it have enough problems of its own?) and to share added money with virtual competitors (wouldn't it be better to give any additional money directly to each separate unit?) But the idea caught on. Libraries evidently were looking for ways to gain access to greater resources, and participation in a system gave them this opportunity without requiring them to give up local prerogatives. In the twenty-five years after World War II, most states developed some kind of interlibrary system organization. A survey in 1969 found 491 systems in the country.[12]

One of the advantages of the systems concept was that it could take a variety of forms, and therefore could apply to very different circumstances. At its simplest and most frequent level it took the form of a "*cooperative*" unit made up of two or more nearby libraries. No change was made in formal or legal organization, and no additional unit or level was added to the picture. The participating libraries could agree to such joint ventures as the following and could do so step by step: reciprocal borrowing privileges, with residents using whichever library they choose; interlibrary loan, with rapid (usually daily) delivery of requested materials; return of borrowed publications at any one of the participating libraries; the sharing recently of access to computerized data systems. From the users standpoint, the result was access to an expanded body of resources while still retaining their local libraries.

As a further stage of systems development, a group of cooperating libraries could establish an office and structure to administer the joint ventures and to provide some central services, thus creating a *"coordinated"* system. This required formal action by boards of directors or other government bodies, while still retaining the local libraries with their own administrators. The coordinated structure facilitated such further joint actions as union catalogs of holdings of the member agencies, centralized processing, and in-service training of staffs. In some cases the coordinated system designated one agency within the group to be a "central" library, a relatively stronger collection to which all residents of the systems area had access and full use. This more formal structure often came about because of encouragement by state library consultants and with the stimulus of state aid. Finally there was the possibility of outright combination of existing units into a new entity with one legal board and one administrator, thus creating a *"consolidated"* system. This did not happen frequently, for the simple reason that it brought the cycle back to the reluctance of libraries once established to give up their identity and independence.

In some states with more advanced structures, an additional or intermediate level of facility has appeared—that is, intermediate between the local system and the central state library. Terms for the facility at this level vary, sometimes they are called resource centers or research coordinators. They differ from systems because they cover much larger areas and—most importantly—include not only public libraries but also college and university units, and special research collections, and even in some cases bringing school libraries into the fold. Their emphasis is on research resources and services. Here again state money is important. This intermediate level not only improves the range of materials available through local libraries but also improves resources to bear upon business and industrial development and upon advanced needs in scientific and medical research. Here is where pioneering work in application of telecommunication and in access to computerized data and the Internet can be accomplished. Call these *networks* as distinct from the smaller and more circumscribed systems.

The development of systems and networks in New York State illustrates this trend at an advanced level. New York has no less than 740 local public libraries; only 104 (14 percent) serve 25,000 people or more—294 (40 percent) serve less than 5,000 people. These 740 agencies are organized into 23 systems (the smallest serving 160,000 people), and nine intermediate networks.[13] At the peak is the state library, the "library's library." The total structure is supported to the extent of thirty dollars per capita, 72 percent coming from local tax money, 10 percent from state aid, and the remainder from private sources.

The systems movement spread further across the country in the 1970s and 1980s, taking different forms in different states. By the end of the century the criticism of an inadequate governmental base for public-library service had to be modified. To a degree the total resources of the country had been combined in a kind of national system. Most users entering their local facility, no matter how small, now usually have access to a wider world of resources through systems and networks and their state libraries. That is, they have this access if they know how to use the system and if their local library takes steps to show them that it is there.

A few examples will show how the idea works out in different settings, one a rural district and the other a metropolitan area. Examples could be extended through many variations and combinations.

The North Central Regional Library in the middle of the state of Washington serves five counties with a total area of 14,940 square miles, larger than the state of Massachusetts. The total population is about 100,000. It is a modified consolidated system with a single, overall administration, held together by contracts with small existing libraries that have a degree of independence. There is a single trustee board with members appointed by the commissioners of the five counties. Actually the system grew directly from a demonstration project operated by the state in the 1960s, using federal Library Service Act funds for the purpose. In time the local voters supported the demonstration and provided local funds to carry on the service. However, financial support has been a problem over the years.

The area is predominately rural, with the largest city, Wenatchee, under 20,000 in population. It is a productive fruit-growing area with apples being the predominant crop. Distances are great, and this has been a problem factor from the beginning. At the same time it is not an isolated or backward area, for the metropolitan center of Seattle is one hundred miles to the west, over the Cascade Mountains.

When the demonstration project began, 40 percent of the area lacked library service and most provision in the centers was substandard. A regional system was built up, based on Wenatchee. Branches were established in several of the smaller centers, and three bookmobiles carried books to more remote locations. Collections of books were circulated among the various units, children's books prominent among them. A reference and referral system was established going through Wenatchee and on to the state library. Training was instituted for local staff. People responded: home circulation of books rose from 392,903 to 1,040,470, higher than in many urban areas and also higher than in many rural districts.

The North Central Regional Library is an example of the systems or larger-unit concept bringing reading materials to a predominantly rural area. It also demonstrates what a small amount of outside money can accomplish in pulling localities into joint effort. The district was ready and eager and responded to the stimulus. How many lives have been changed or affected cannot be documented, but the system has clearly made a difference.

A very different and much larger example is Monroe County and its Pioneer Library System in the Rochester area in New York.[14] This five-county unit serving over a million people was built in the 1960s and 1970s, primarily under the initiative of the director of the Rochester Public Library. This is a hybrid because individual libraries participated voluntarily in the plan (fifty-eight such units at one point); there is also a central coordinating facility, and the whole system is held together by legal contracts. All of the possibilities of cooperation have been brought into play: reciprocal borrowing, interlibrary loan and daily delivery, a union catalog, centralized processing, and joint planning and staff training.

A few unusual features must be mentioned. When the Monroe County unit was added along the way, the director of the city library also became director of the county entity. Now the county finances the central facility, which is open to all residents in the system area. And, due to revisions in the state-aid program in

New York State, the system has since broken into two pieces—the Monroe County Library and the Pioneer Library System for the four surrounding counties. In any case this example demonstrates what can be accomplished with state-aid money and also testifies to what can be accomplished by an enterprising and diplomatic library administrator, Harold Hacker in this case.

It would be overly sanguine to conclude that the systems concept has removed all limitations and problems of the governmental organization of public library service in the United States. There are still many people who have only their own isolated unit to turn to for service (and still several million without any local facilities). Despite a century of growth, these people find themselves dependent on a small library that has limited connection with a larger world of recorded knowledge, an agency that has no chance of coming up to reasonable standards. Call them one-room libraries, comparable to one-room schools.

But the idea of working together in multijurisdictional systems has put many more millions in touch with this larger world. You can live on a farm in a small town, or in a suburb and not be cut off from the record on the printed page or stored in a computer. It is to the credit of library administrators that they have been ready to step across jurisdictional lines and cooperate with their colleagues to achieve what they could not do alone.

## The Library in the Community

Perhaps the title for this section should be "The Library Out in the Community" or "The Community Brought into the Library." The topic is the relationship between the local library and its locality. Over the years a foundation of service had been built, starting with a basic subject collection, supplemented by reference and information provision, extending to recreational materials, and featuring distinctive children's service. According to the Public Library Inquiry; this standard pattern appealed to a portion of the population, the better educated portion, and usually the portion more established economically—what can loosely be called the "middle class." As we have seen (see section on Use and Users in the 1946–60 period), this responding group amounted to less than one-half of the population.

From early on librarians sought to reach more of the people. A missionary spirit animated part of their work. They would take part of the facilities out to people, or they would organize new activities to bring people into the center. The term used in the literature was usually "outreach." How successful were the missionary efforts—how many converts were made?

The outreach efforts began near the beginning of the century. One of the first was branch libraries outside from the center of the city. It was clear that some potential users would not make the effort to go to the central facility but would respond to a collection within a mile or less of their homes. Further, branches provided an opportunity to adjust resources and activities to different neighborhoods, from affluent sections to manufacturing and industrial areas, from neighborhoods with foreign-born residents to traditional middle-class communities. Separate branches could be organized to serve business interests.

When branch librarians first appeared, automobile ownership was quite uncommon. But branches soon acquired local public support and the agencies stayed on even when transportation became more convenient. This can hardly be attributed to the unique programs developed in neighborhoods, because most of these outlying units seem to be pressed from one mold. No, the determining factor was convenience, the nearby location versus the more distant centers; convenience plus local pride.

The policy of outlying branch libraries was a distinct success. Individuals and families turned to them. The local units became part of community life. Even to this day—with automobiles in almost every family and expressways in almost every city—the branch libraries persist. Business has centralized (and now decentralized) and retail trade is concentrated in malls, but the local community branch remains. Protest is likely if branch libraries are closed due to budget restraints. Whether branches have reached a different segment of the population is a moot point; they certainly attract more patronage in middle-level communities.

The service organization created in the 1920s—to serve children, young adults, adult information inquiries, and adult education—were forms of outreach aimed at segments of the population. Several of these also caught on and continue to characterize the institution at the end of the century. The exceptions are young adult and distinct adult education activities, which have faded somewhat into the background. In the foreground now are the cultural mission (basic collection), information service (reference collection and staff), recreation (fiction and best-sellers) and children's materials and services; this is the enduring core.

Another early effort arose from the flood of immigrants entering the country in the early decades. The public library sought to mobilize its resources to help the newcomers to prepare for citizenship and employment, in the form of Americanization classes. This was not easy because of the language barrier, which librarians tried to bridge with materials in foreign languages and in simplified English. Unresolved was the question of whether this program worked against the goal of cultural pluralism. This formal and concentrated effort did not last very long, because formal classwork was outside the mainstream of library service and because the immigrants in time became assimilated.

Over the years, reaching people in the ever-increasing under-privileged parts of cities has been a concern of public librarians. The slum areas have increased while the public library became entrenched in other parts of the metropolis. This was not readily accomplished in the run-down neighborhoods, but not for lack of trying. Librarians tried different approaches, with simplified texts, with films, with book discussions, even with handicrafts. The children can be reached, and teenagers to some extent, but adults only occasionally. It is hard to break through the lack of connection and motivation; the underprivileged do not see the library as an agency suited to them. This may be changing somewhat as minority groups shift to helping themselves rather than depending on outside services and agencies.

This problem is so important that it is worth giving a little attention to a few efforts to reach beyond the middle-class, educated groups that make up the bulk of library users. In the late 1930s the Chicago Public Library established an experimental branch in South Chicago, an Eastern European working-class neighborhood in the shadow of large steel mills. Books were selected that stressed practical local matters such as home repair and gardening, cooking and health and raising children, and the material was shelved in interest groupings rather than in the usual Dewey Decimal arrangement. Emphasis was placed on film material. Deposit stations were placed in the steel mills. Contact with local ethnic groups brought out a limited number of local leaders who proceeded to work with the library. What was surprising was the positive reaction from some local union groups. It took a little extra fortitude to stand in front of a union meeting, have someone in the front row shout "We don't want to hear about the library—let's get on with union business," and still persist by holding up a pamphlet on organizing and tell the protester that he should read it. There was also an unexpected response from young people to drama groups based on library materials, evidently an outlet for expression not provided by other agencies or groups in this lower middle-class community.

The Queens Public Library tried a more radical approach in the 1950s. A new library branch that was housed in an empty storefront was put into the control of a local committee. Staff was recruited not from library schools but from the local area. Local artists competed to design the signs for the establishment. The unit did not have the usual subject collection found in other branches. Materials were selected about local needs and problems. Pamphlets were obtained in quantity and given out free to users; substantial numbers of leaflets about health problems, employment opportunities, legislative issues and educational facilities were distributed. There were a few shelves of recreational reading, not bestsellers but mystery stories, westerns, and romances. Each day after school there were homework sessions for children. The experiment got enough attention that it drew a visit from the mayor of New York City. Today the Queens Library is reaching out to newly arrived Asian residents.

It would be overly optimistic to conclude that these and other experiments bridged the gap to low-education communities. This endeavor confronts a whole compound of backgrounds, abilities, motivations and hang-ups, on the part of both staff and potential users. The middle-class respectability of the library gets in the way. An advocate of outreach to minorities stated that "We have seen some notable if sporadic forays in the past, but the true battle has hardly been joined, much less won."[15]

Even with the usual library clientele, libraries large and small have used a wide range of come-ons to attract specific sections of the community: film showings, lectures, book sales, craft shows, art exhibits, income-tax advice, etc. "Friends" groups have gotten into the act: The Friends of the San Francisco Public Library have an annual author lecture which attracts hundreds of people who pay an admission fee. The Friends of the Ticonderoga (New York) Public Library put on a free lecture series given by local college faculty members, who are lucky if they get an audience of two dozen people.

More novel efforts were tried occasionally. One was bibliotherapy, the application of reading to problems of emotional instability, loneliness, and alienation, but librarians were not really trained for this activity. Some libraries carried books out to shut-ins and residents of institutions. Program planning institutes to bring local groups together were tried in Baltimore and Detroit. Great books discussion groups met in a variety of libraries.

At times it seems that the public library is trying to be the community center. This of course is not its function. It is seeking to reach out, to relate to its constituency. Usually it falls back on activities that connect with its basic resources, the record of knowledge that is its reason for being.

Different librarians have reacted differently to these various attempts to reach out to or bring in elements in the community. Some professionals, restless with the standard program and critical of the passive nature of the public library, embraced these fresh attempts and received satisfaction from the limited results obtained. Margaret Monroe was a champion of this group and she made a strong case for reaching out.[16] Other librarians, including many longtime administrators, looked with skepticism on these extraordinary community efforts and concentrated on the essential goals of improving collections and strengthening reference service. Essentially they rested easy with the basic program of service and with the portion of the population that had been reached. In any case, time was on the side of the latter group, as budgets tightened in the 1990s, increasing demands were made for computerized information, and community outreach had to be curtailed.

It is notable that the public library has retained its local community base throughout the century, despite the changes in the organization of American life. Within cities, local neighborhoods have struggled to hold on to viable community connections. Outside of cities, new affiliations have emerged in the growth of suburbs.

Whether within the city or in the new towns round about, the libraries became part of the community structure, and were conceived as such by local residents. They were usually located somewhere in or adjacent to the nearby business districts that had grown over the years. They had local boards or advisory committees, and in addition often established Friends of the Library groups. Some had meeting facilities that were used by local groups. They were an integral part of community life; the localities would be weakened if they were for some reason to close.

Then in recent decades the decline of city neighborhoods continued as did also the cohesiveness of some suburbs. An important factor in this change was the growing concentration of shopping facilities, with larger malls taking over the retail functions previously provided in local centers. The growing popularity of automobiles furthered the change.

What is left back at the previous center? There may be a few local stores, the churches remain and nearby schools, the town hall in the suburbs—and the public library. In the face of centralization and decentralization, the library continues to be one tie that binds. The agency started as a community facility, and it remains as such at the end of the century.

The loosening of community cohesion continues. This raises the question of what the affiliation of the public library should be and can be in the next century. Will enough of community life remain to provide a suitable setting for the agency? Will concentrations in retail malls and office parks continue to the point where the local public library should consider relocation? Or will electronic provision of information and communication, from individual to database, progress to the point where the public library as we have known it is no longer necessary?

Time will provide the answers. The prediction of this history is that the public library has sufficient community roots and enough of a monopoly on part of individual communication to remain in some form in the years ahead—that is, if it has enough resiliency to change with the times.

## Multimedia Provision

The library has often been called an agency of communication, whether the communication is in book or nonbook form. As more and more new media appeared, particularly after the middle of the century, the public library sought to become a multimedia agency. To what extent has it suceeded? What is its role in the world of multiforms of communication?

Currently we are said to be coming into the Information Age. We have actually been in a Communication Age for decades. Want to know how to fix your toilet? Read a book, get a microfilm of a journal article, listen to a tape cassette, view a video film—or call a plumber, and use old-fashioned direct human communication. The simple choice would seem to be the plumber, but you probably will have to wait and you certainly will get a bill. The many different forms of multimedia communication have each entered into the program of the public library.

Starting from the traditional base of the book, there are the other print forms, the magazine and the pamphlet. Public libraries have accepted and embraced the periodical form, the magazine and journal. They provide display space for magazines, keep back issues, either bound or in microfilm, and some provide periodical rooms or alcoves, sometimes with easy chairs. A medium-sized library has several hundred subscriptions, which cost $10,000 annually, and a large public library will have several thousand subscriptions. Speaking in broad terms, the periodical collection may be said to have roughly the same subject range and level as the book collection, appealing to about the same range of users. The public library has accepted responsibility for providing access to magazines and journals, for these fit neatly into its traditional mission.

The same categorical statement cannot be made for pamphlets and reports, which in a sense are small books without stiff covers. There is seldom an organized and systematic program for locating and acquiring this material. Once it is in hand, it goes into file drawers, usually without receiving an entry into the catalog, and is filed under subject headings that may not be known to the user. A weeding program to get rid of outdated material may or may not exist. Use of the pamphlet file is sporadic at best, usually as a backup if suitable book content is not found in the collection. Here is the first of the media that has not really been fully adopted into the family.

The very largest public libraries may handle still another form of non-book printed material, government documents. Over 1,000 such libraries (public and academic) are included in the system of depositories over the country that provide distribution for publications of federal offices, in order to keep citizens informed about the working of the federal government. This responsibility imposes a burden on the library to provide space and staff. To this point we have what could be called a multiprint agency.

An allied resource is pictorial material. Illustrations of course are incorporated into books and may be consulted there for information and understanding. A very few public libraries have developed pictorial collections, which are a resource for journalists, business interests, and students in specialized fields. A notable example is the collection of the New York Public Library at Lincoln Center. Most public libraries have found separate pictorial resources (photographs, prints, drawings, posters) beyond their physical capacity and their expertise.

Shifting from print and images on paper, there is an abundance of audio materials. The earliest to appear with any prominence in public libraries were sound recordings, first in disc and later in tape form. Acceptance of audio materials marked a distinct step for the library, for it was moving beyond print to a very different medium. A survey in 1968 of medium-sized and larger public libraries found that 40 percent had record collections in some form,[17] and the number of participating agencies increased after that as long-playing records came into vogue. The provision is by no means universal. Some smaller libraries may have only a few hundred discs while most city libraries are likely to have several thousand. Circulation was substantial for twenty years or so after World War II but has fallen off somewhat in recent years. Both radio and television have been factors in the decline of use of recordings from libraries. Young people are the largest group of audio material users today — and young people are not the most regular of users of public libraries.

The audio forms are of many different types and deal with varied subject matter. Besides music, both classical and popular, there are recordings for language study, drama, poetry, and recordings of speeches by public figures. Most recently books are also in audio form. Most libraries provide open access to the material, following the pattern for books, and they are ingenious in devising ways for displaying and organizing recordings, some even placing the discs adjacent to books on the same topics.

Larger libraries might have recording and replay studios, and many have earphones available for listening to materials in the building. Currently the emphasis is more on audiotapes; discs are standing relatively unused on the shelves.

Reaching out to audio forms added to the public librariy's multimedia character. People come to the agency for recordings for many of the same reasons that they come for books—to locate a specific item, to browse among materials to their liking, even to do reference work. This consultation cannot be said to constitute the bulk of use of sound materials. Retail outlets provide for more of the listening sources, while libraries have this material more as a sideshow, supplementing their basic function of providing book resources.

The motion-picture film industry grew with the public library during the twentieth century, from *The Great Train Robbery* of 1903, through *The Birth of a Nation* (1915), on to Charlie Chaplin in *The Gold Rush* (1925) and the advent of sound with Al Jolson in *The Jazz Singer* (1927). Not long after sound came color. Since then there have been western films and gangster movies and spy films and historical pictures and cartoons from Disney, and many others, including documentary and instructional films on literally thousands of topics. First the movie palaces and then the nearby television set have carried this multimedia marvel of sight and sound. It is a rare American who does not see a film on his or her television set every week—indeed, for some almost every day—and in addition at intervals they go out to a movie house to see (and hear) the newest release.

In the early years the library moved slowly and cautiously into the provision of film. Very few users had the equipment to show sixteen millimeter film at home; organizations might have projectors and screens, and larger libraries provided some material for them. But in time came the flood of video cassettes which could be played through the VCR attachment to the home television set. Now even relatively small libraries have at least a few cassettes and large libraries may devote a whole room to them. The compact cassettes can be placed on shelves like books. There are the early films for historical reference, the greatest movies of previous years, the current releases and also the instructional films on everything from repairing the automobile to traveling to Africa. A few libraries went further and actually started workshops in which enrollees learned how to direct and make films.[18]

Film material is used quite steadily in public libraries. However, the agency is in competition with the "free show" that can be seen on television every evening, and there also is the retail lending source with its stock of current releases. The library is one among several players, and many people do not think first of the agency when they seek diversion or want to see the newest release. Like sound records, the visual media have been a supplement to the basic book collection, a colorful adornment to the holdings for which the institution exists.

Microforms have been incorporated more readily into library resources. Of course microfilm and microfiche are, strictly speaking, not new media but are copies in reduced format of printed pages. Because the essential content is familiar, librarians do not have to make so much of an adjustment, even though the typical user may be uncertain about the format and less than comfortable with the machine in which it must be projected. But microfilm has prevailed because the advantage of its reduced size and reduced storage space. It was used by public libraries when they first appeared in the 1950s and 1960s, first for files of newspapers and then for previous runs of periodicals. These days even somewhat smaller agencies have at least one microfilm reader and larger libraries need a bank of machines because demand is substantial. Many microfilm projectors even have a built-in printer, so that users can have a full-size copy, bringing them back to the original medium, words on a page. Predictions were made that microforms would become the primary medium for new information in libraries,[19] but this was before computer databases came into existence.

One of the problems of multimedia provision is to determine how to coordinate the several forms so that the user gets the benefit of each and supplementing the other. One can go into a public library seeking material about President John F. Kennedy and go out with a biography in book form, an audiocassette of one of his speeches, and a film on the 1960s. But this is uncommon. Public libraries have not found ways to coordinate and mobilize the various media for enriched understanding, nor have they developed or utilized audio-visual learning (teaching) programs. You can go into a library and put together a multimedia package on a topic of interest, but the public library (unlike the school library or bookstore) does not provide access to prepared packages. This is an indication of the distance that the public library has moved from its earlier advisory function, for the current learning programs are similar to the reading courses put together by reader's advisers in the 1920s and 1930s.

This brief survey identified two non-book forms which the public library adopted and made an integral part of the collection: periodicals and microfilm. Essentially these provided what the book collection did, print on a page or screen. No basic adjustment was necessary on the part of librarians to select and utilize these two forms. The same was not true for other audio-visual materials: audio discs and tapes, films, and visual cassettes. Here the content is conveyed by the new forms, they are based on a different technology, and call for unfamiliar standards for judgment. As a result much of the multimedia provision in libraries is seen by the professionals as an adjunct to their basic resource, the book collection, materials interesting and unique in their own right but occupying a subordinate or supplementary position. They have their own methods for physical handling, they require intervening machines for communication, and mostly have a separate group of users. For the general public the public library is not seen as the natural or predominant source for sound and visual media.

This situation prompted one of the most insightful of multimedia advocates to conclude that the American public library is "becoming an anachronism."[20] This harsh judgment was made in 1971; more than a quarter century later the institution is still with us and apparently thriving. The public library must have something that protects and sustains its social value—could it be the old-fashioned, nonmedia book collection?

## Measurement and Evaluation

Evaluation is an integral part of administration, indeed the culmination of the management process. After plans have been set, staff hired, jobs described, and work completed, the question is how well an enterprise has done, how close it has come to the objectives adopted.

Most services have built-in evaluation. Business has the bottom line of profits. The doctor knows whether the patient recovers or dies, the lawyer knows whether the case is won or lost, the teacher knows whether the students have achieved or failed. In each case they have a measure of success, and more than that they can examine the results and improve their further ministrations.

Theoretically libraries also have built-in measures. Does the user get the document sought—does he or she get the information requested? However, libraries have no regular answers, nor do they go out of their way to determine the results. The library is organized to deliver, but it does not know whether it delivers or not. The librarian shoots an arrow into the air and knows not where it lands.

Several facts and circumstances account for this lack of evaluation and feedback. The relationship between staff member and user is usually impersonal and discontinuous; the librarian seldom stays with seekers long enough to learn whether their searches are successful or not. Users are not inclined to complain, because the library provides services free of charge and is clearly trying to serve. It is unusual for a library to ask for any report from readers when they leave or even to have a suggestion box. Most do not have criteria which would enable them to make a judgment. Finally, particularly in public libraries, the objectives —an educated public, informed citizens, adults who appreciate culture—would be most difficult to measure; in fact some critics have raised the question of whether libraries have any right to determine the result of the use of library materials: "What the user subsequently does with these materials is completely outside the librarian's control (and, some users might say, none of the librarian's business)."[21] Both the librarian and the public proceed on faith—faith in the value of the book or the document, and faith in the value of accurate information. This is what motivates librarians and this is what prompts government officials to approve budget requests.

Despite the complexity of the exercise, in the 1960s and 1970s librarians made efforts to evaluate their institution. For public libraries this was given a push forward by a challenging publication by De Prospo[22] in which he stressed measuring outcomes or results rather than traditional library inputs. This was followed by a manual for applying the same approach.[23] In actual investigations, attention was given more to parts of the library program—evaluation of collections, of catalogs, and of reference service—and not to end results in terms of requests fulfilled and users satisfied. Emphasis was more on inputs and less on outcomes.

For collections the measures used were size, rate of growth, expenditures, and rate of circulation.[24] Criticisms come readily to mind for each of these criteria. A collection of 100,000 volumes may be no better than a collection of 50,000 if the former has not been weeded regularly and still holds outdated and unused material; indeed it may be less appropriate. Similarly, a collection that lacks a substantial representation of recent titles may be less useful than one that has kept up with the current output. In using annual expenditure as a measure, does the money go into duplicates or into variety of acquisitions? Circulation may come closer to the mark, because actual use is involved, but this may tell more about the users than about the holdings. Still another approach is to check holdings against a standard list, such as the *Standard Catalog for Public Libraries*, but this assumes that the compilers of the list and the local library had the same objectives and clientele in mind. Efforts to combine such measures to get a more definitive appraisal have not been very successful. Libraries are still short of that evaluation that would permit an overall judgment of the agency.

Work on card catalog use has been done more on academic than on public libraries as in *The Catalog Use Study of ALA* in 1958,[25] and similar research at the University of Michigan (1970),[26] Yale University (1972),[27] and the University of Chicago (1972).[28] The methods used were observation or interviews, or both, of users at the catalog in sample periods. In the ALA study (four thousand interviews, including a small number in public libraries) 66 percent of the known item searches and 80 percent of the subject searches were successful. The first of these of course is more a measure of collections than of catalogs. To help in subject searches it was found that more "see" references were needed to direct searchers to headings actually used in the catalogs. The success rates seemed to satisfy the researchers, but failure of one-third of the title seekers and one-fifth of the subject seekers is still a cause for concern. Beyond these studies within particular environments is the question of whether the standard cataloging practices, which apply in markedly different kinds of libraries, are suitable for users as different as students in schools, for the general public in public libraries, and advanced researchers in subject fields. The question applies to traditional card catalogs and also to computerized catalogs which afford greater variety and combination of entries, assuming that users can learn to use the greater capacity of on-line records. To evaluate reference services, more work has been done on the public-library side.[29] Some crude information can be gained in any library simply by counting the number of questions asked, along with the librarian's opinion of how many were answered correctly. In practice, libraries that keep such records often discontinue doing so after a period, attesting to the low motivation that librarians have for self-evaluation. Further insight can be obtained by periodic observation by supervisors of what goes on at the reference desk in sample periods. Supervisors must note the extent to which the reference librarians clarify the original inquiry, their knowledge of and skill in using reference sources, and the extent of follow-up done to determine whether the demand was satisfied.

Closer to the heart of the matter was the use of "unobtrusive" research into the actual responses from a variety of libraries. Terence Crowley developed a method of using actual questions asked in public libraries, and giving these to "sample shoppers" who asked the questions anonymously in person or by telephone in selected libraries and who recorded the responses.[30] The results were not encouraging. In general only half of the inquiries were answered correctly. The promising Crowley technique gained attention and was used by a few other investigators, but then fell by the wayside, attesting once again to librarians' disinclination to examine themselves.

One form of evaluation that has been used consistently is appraisal of staff. Many libraries prepare annual reviews of staff performance, and they may use these in counseling personnel and occasionally in decisions on promotions. Three different approaches are possible: appraisal by traits, appraisal by behavior, and appraisal by outcomes. The first refers to characteristics of individuals that are usually considered necessary for job performance, such as reliability, responsibility, cooperativeness, loyalty, and friendliness. The individual is observed by the supervisor and his or her judgment is recorded on some form of rating scale. Appraisal by performance is much less common but can be gained by observation at the work station, the circulation desk, or the reference desk. Least common is appraisal by outcomes—that is, accuracy of catalog entries, for example, or degree of satisfaction of inquirers for information. Presumably the totality of staff evaluations would go a long way toward appraisal of the whole agency, but the separate staff judgments are seldom projected to get some indication of overall success or failure.

One special method for evaluating personnel is to get the combined judgment of other staff members—appraisal by peer opinion. This is used widely in colleges and universities, where tenured faculty decide whether a candidate for tenure is approved or not. A variation of this could be used in libraries, with senior professionals deciding whether juniors should be promoted or not. This has seldom occurred in libraries because it could arouse personal friction within the staff.

Beyond straight appraisal of a service is the question of cost-effectiveness. Assuming that a library did determine that its efforts have achieved its objectives, the next question is whether it was worth the cost. This carries the matter into rough and uncharted seas. Complex value judgments would be involved. Given the fact that libraries have not ventured very far in evaluation, it is not surprising that one searches in vain for cost-effective studies in the field.

In general, public libraries have not tried to evaluate the success or failure of what they do. A combination of reasons account for this lack of taking the culminating step of administration. To begin with, objectives are broad and grand, and not very measurable. Neither administrators nor staff have wanted to subject themselves to such analysis. If they were so motivated, they would have to turn to users by some means, and library users are not inclined to pass judgment or to register complaints, even though they have just been frustrated in a search for books or information. The users themselves would be uncertain because they generally have no standards or criteria by which to judge a given library.

Granting all these problems, it would still be possible to get some response. Users leaving the library could be presented with a simple question: did they get what they came for, and why not? Studies we have show that library patrons are willing to respond; they respect the library enough to take the time and effort. This could be done either by questionnaire or in person. The feedback would be mostly positive and favorable, but there would be some sizable gaps and shortcomings. The agency would be better for having considered them and taking steps for improvement.

In conclusion, some effort has been made by librarians to evaluate their efforts, but this has not become regularly ingrained in library administration and, therefore, has had little impact on the agency.

## Notes

1. Betty Freidan, *The Feminine Mystique.* (New York: Norton, 1963).
2. Diane Ravitch, *The Troubled Crusade.* (New York: Basic Books, 1983), 297.
3. Edward G. Holley, *The Library Services and Construction Act.* (Greenwich, Conn.: JAI Press, 1983), 18.
4. Ibid, 58.
5. Ibid, 69–70.
6. Ibid, 75.
7. *ALA Washington Newsletter* 11 March, 1966, 1–2.
8. *ALA Washington Newsletter* 21 July, 1966, 1–2.
9. Edward Holley, *Library Services,* 80.
10. Carleton B. Joeckel and Amy Winslow, *A National Plan for Public Library Service* (Chicago: American Library Association, 1948), 50.
11. Robert D. Leigh, *The Public Library in the United States* (New York: Columbia University Press, 1950).
12. Nelson Associates, *Public Library Systems in the United States* (Chicago: American Library Association, 1969), 25.
13. New York State Library, *Public and Association Library Statistics* (Albany, N.Y.: State Education Department, 1990), VII.
14. Interview with Harold Hacker, director emeritus of the Rochester Public Library, 2 February, 1996.
15. Hardy Franklin, "Service to the Urban Rank and File" in *A Century of Service,* ed. Sidney L. Jackson (Chicago: American Association, 1976), 17.
16. Margaret E. Monroe, "Emerging Patterns of Community Service." *Library Trends,* vol. 28 (1979–80), 121–337.
17. Eric Cooper, "Gramophone Record Libraries in the United States of America," in Margaret Chisholm, ed. *Reader in Media, Technology and Libraries.* (Englewood, Colo.: Microcard Editions Book, 1975), 76.
18. Margaret Chisholm, *Reader in Media,* 128–33.
19. Klaus W. Otten, "An Hypothesis: Microform Will Become the

Major Medium for New Information in Reference Libraries," *Micrographics* vol. (1971), 265–73.

20. C. Walter Stone, "The Use of Media and Technology," in Margaret Chisholm, *Reader in Media*, 201.

21. F. W. Lancaster, T*he Measurement and Evaluation of Library Services* (Washington, D.C.: Information Resources Press, 1977), 4.

22. Ernest De Prospo, *Performance Measures for Public Libraries.* (Chicago: American Library Association, 1973).

23. Douglas Zweizig, *Output Measures for Public Libraries: A Manual of Standardized Procedures* (Chicago: American Library Association, 1982)

24. George S. Bonn, "Evaluation of the Collection," Library Trends, vol. 22 (1974), 265–304.

25. American Library Association, *Catalog Use Study* (Chicago: The American Library Association, 1958).

26. R. Tagliacozzo, "Access and Recognition: From Users' Data to Catalogue Entries." *Journal of Documentation* vol. 26 (1970), 230–49.

27. Ben-ami Lipetz, "Catalog Use in a Large Research Library." *Library Quarterly*, vol. 42 (1972), 129–39.

28. D. R. Swanson, "Requirements Study for Future Catalogs." *Library Quarterly*, vol. 42 (1972), 302–15.

29. Samuel Rothstein, "The Measurement and Evaluation of Reference Service." *Library Trends*, vol. 12 (1964), 456–72.

30. Terence Crowley and Thomas Childers, *Information Service in Public Libraries: Two Studies*. (Metuchen, N.J.: Scarecrow Press, 1971).

# 7

# The Culminating Years, 1980–1999

America entered the last two decades of the century in high gear. Industrial production increased, consumption mounted, and the standard of living went up even further. Fifteen million automobiles were sold each year; at the Four Seasons Restaurant in New York City you could get a serving of choice caviar for ninety dollars. The stock market went up and up. With Ronald Reagan in the White House stability prevailed in the society even though the national deficit increased. The cold war with the Soviet Union eased off along with the nuclear threat.

The 1990s should have been the best of times, but there were danger signals, cracks appeared in the foundation, and disillusion and skepticism spread across the land. The visible signs come first to mind: violence and crime, the poor and homeless, AIDS and drugs. At a deeper level two basic institutions showed weaknesses. Perhaps the deepest crack in the foundation occurred in the family. Half of marriages in the nineties ended in divorce. Births to unwed mothers increased. Many children were growing up without the guidance and discipline of close-knit families and communities.

In 1992 the long period of Republican control of the presidency came to an end with the election of Bill Clinton. Then the electorate turned around and elected many Republicans to the Congress in 1994. Two years later came another reversal with the reelection of Clinton.

President Clinton and Vice President Al Gore frequently express an interest in electronic access to information and have proposed that every library and school be connected to the Internet. The president mentioned libraries in his 1997 State of the Union address, but the 1998 federal budget provides limited funds for the purpose. What money is available under the 1996 Library Services and Technology Act (which replaced the Library Services and Construction Act) will be administered by a newly created Institute of Museum and Library Services, a small offshoot that can be lost among the larger federal agencies.

A continuing controversy has to do with the role of government. Starting back in the depression years and on into the time of the Great Society, government—and particularly the federal government—was seen as a service agency, there to help people realize their potential (schools, libraries), there as a safety net to rescue the poor and the under-educated (welfare, social services), there to help in old age (Social Security, Medicare), there to protect individuals (testing of drugs and consumer products), and there to regulate business when necessary. But this ideology was challenged in the nineties. "Get the government off our backs," said the critics. "Return such activities to the states and localities." Public libraries were caught between the two views. In the push and pull of these conflicting views, cities were strapped for funds and library budgets were cut before the balanced budgets of the 1990s.

Add other disruptions. Downsizing in business has become the aim; the first two sentences of a report in the *Wall Street Journal* read "Last week Mobil corporation posted soaring first-quarter profits. This week it announced plans to eliminate 4,700 jobs." The welcoming and absorption of immigrants had marked the growth of the United States; now restrictions were placed on immigration and warnings issued that the fabric of American life was being weakened by newcomers.[1] A safety net for poor people had been maintained; now welfare was being challenged on all sides. Affirmative action has been used to help minorities move into the mainstream; now this was generally criticized and (in California) legally attacked as a policy of inequality. The emergence of private antigovernment militias, with guns and camouflage suits and military maneuvers did not help the situation. In every aspect of society, both policies and values were being challenged.

Some doomsayers examining the cracks in the foundation have predicted the fall of the structure. Paul Kennedy, drawing on extensive historical data, points to the eventual problem of "great powers" still carrying economic and military responsibilities on an international scale but facing economic slowdown—the problem of decline and fall.[2] He believes the United States is well along in the cycle.

But present-day evidence is not readily available to support this thesis. In the second half of the final decade, industrial production continues unabated. Unemployment is relatively low. The Dow Jones average index of the stock prices reached 3,000 in 1980, 4,000 by 1990, and over 9,000 before the end of the decade. This does not seem like the fall of the American empire.

Nor is the general pessimism shared by the many spectators who attended 3,389 performances of *Chorus Line* on Broadway. Nor by the crowds standing in line to see exhibits of impressionist paintings. Nor by enthusiasts working over their personal computers. Nor by the increasing numbers of older people living beyond seventy-five and even beyond eighty-five.

By 1990 computerization had moved beyond the office and the research center to enter individual homes—and libraries. Personal computers are now used for financial records, correspondence, business data, even recipes and golf records. A vast new world of communication has opened on the Internet. It remains only to peer into the crystal ball to see what these developments portend for libraries.

The book longest on the bestseller lists in the 1990s was *The Bridges of Madison County*, the turgid account of a murky four-day love affair between a repressed farm wife and an itinerant photographer, highlighted by a sex scene on the kitchen floor. The number of outstanding titles was relatively small in these final years. As always, critics held up the society for view: *The Color Purple* (1982), *Bonfire of the Vanities* (1987), *There Are No Children Here* (1991), *The Disuniting America* (1992), *The Sibling Society* (1996).

While the sale of books increased steadily in the 1990s, and superbookstores appeared, the publishing industry worried about the future of the book. The Book-of-the-Month Club dropped its panel of judges and looked more toward the advertising campaigns mounted by publishers and toward sales figures in making its choices.

What is the prospect at the end of the century? Has Nirvana been achieved, so that we will go through the next hundred years growing in industry, comfortable with our many products, and getting our satisfaction from consumption? Or are the goals and principles refined over many decades now coming under critical view, and if this is occurring, what will be the new credo? What mission will sustain the next generations? No clear or simple answers emerge from this brief review of our times and of one of its institutions.

Remarkable changes have occurred in the twentieth century. At the end this is a different country from what it was in the beginning—different technologically, economically, politically, and socially. The remaining links are capitalism and democracy, the force that drives and the force that combines. So long as these hold, we have a future.

## Overview of Library Development, 1980–1999

The public library came into the last two decades of the century with considerable strength. It had become a venerable and traditional institution. It was accepted by both the general public and by governmental officials as a standard part of community life. A portion of the adult population continued to turn to it for self-education and for the more substantial of recreational reading. Children—particularly those in the younger years—found it to be a doorway to a larger world recorded in books.

There is some contrast between the two decades. In the 1980s the public library continued on its appointed path with relatively few changes in its service programs. Technological adaptations spread to the point where even smaller agencies had computerized catalogs. By the 1990s developments outside the library in digital storage of data and electronic communication raised basic questions about the role of the institution. Thoughtful administrators wondered about a change in direction, to bring the public library on to the Information Highway, but usually fell back to staying on the existing road.

Financial support kept up with inflation plus a little more during the 1980s but became more stringent in the 1990s. This last did not come about because of a downturn in the economy but more because of an ideological trend in the 1990s to reduce government expenditure and taxes. The federal government cut back on grants to the states for various purposes, this in turn prompted reductions of payments to localities, which included libraries. For example, the mayor of Utica, New York, faced with a large deficit, "proposed the unthinkable—eliminating spending on the Utica Public Library"[3] (actually money was later reinserted in the budget). Library administrators tried to fight back; the head of the New Jersey State Library was dismissed because of reaction against a severe budget cut. The wider political and social change, and the trend toward smaller government proclaimed by both Democrats and Republicans had caught up with the public library. Though this position was really directed against certain aspects of government, such as welfare provision and excessive bureaucracy, it also spilled over to the curtailment of education and related services.

Such threats to financial support came just when the agency was trying to meet the challenge of the Information Age. The public library faced, simultaneously, financial limitation and demands for new services. Was this to be the scenario for the twenty-first century?

The profession fought back on several fronts. New efforts were put into public relations. A fresh approach was made to planning and role setting. The American Library Association adopted a program called Goals 2000 designed to meet oncoming change. The number of computer stations was increased within libraries, more computerized databases were subscribed to, and the sign "Internet" appeared on some of the terminals. With the approach of the expiration of federal financial aid for libraries through the (LSCA), the Library Services and Technology Act was introduced. The selling point would now be libraries' need for technological applications in order to provide wide access to computerized information.

During these years, libraries wrestled with the question of whether to charge for the extensive reference searches being requested by members of the public. To be considered was the long heritage of the public library as a free service—indeed, this was in its very definition. Now with more complex inquiries and with databases that could answer the inquiries if searched by competent staff members, the agency found itself called upon to engage in research that might require a half-hour or more of staff time. Voices were raised on both sides of the issue of whether or not to charge for handling such requests; while charging a fee runs counter to a long tradition, it could attract new clientele in these next years. This might be a forerunner of a future service of the institution, with people lost in the Internet turning to libraries to search out the information they seek. The librarian could be the professional practitioner and expert guide. Even as you turn to a professional lawyer when your affairs become too confused or to a professional doctor when your usual regimen is not working, so you may turn to a professional librarian when you are lost on the Information Highway.

Issues of intellectual freedom were not all in the past. In the 1990s conservative religious groups challenged the public library for having material condoning homosexuality. The new San Francisco central building opened with a room devoted to gay and lesbian literature. The protesters campaigned for what they termed "family-friendly libraries." Consistent with its longtime position, the American Library Association opposed the challenge on the ground that limiting of access to any body of thought constituted censorship. This view was extended to the federal Telecommunications Act of 1996 which sought to protect children from "indecent" material on the Internet.

Construction of library buildings continued. Voters approved bond issues for new structures even when funds for operation were curtailed. Large buildings appeared in Chicago, Phoenix, Denver, San Francisco, and other cities. The basic principles of subject specialization of service and of intermingling of books and readers were retained. Substantial provision was made for book holdings in these new structures, clearly on the assumption that books would continue to have a prominent place over into the twenty-first century. A favorite design feature was the high, open atrium, with service rooms grouped around the open space. The atrium has replaced the monumental stairway as the favored aesthetic feature, and like the stairway it is more visual than functional, for it holds neither books nor services. Rather than new construction, the New York Public Library in 1996 assembled an important Science, Industry and Business Library in a former department store, complete with a million books and workstations for readers with electronic access to databases.

The American Library Association, almost 60,000 strong in membership, adopted Goals 2000 to guide policy into the new century. The emphasis in this manifesto is on fitting libraries into the information culture. The Washington office of ALA has been expanded, a new office for Information Technology Policy has been established, and ALA's Fund for America's Libraries is seeking additional money to further the efforts. The aim is to bring the voice of libraries and librarians into councils and plans for the Digital Age. This commitment to the information side of the library mission may be strategic in view of the national preoccupation with data control, but—as we will see in the final section of this history—the future of the public library may lie as much or more with its longstanding and continuing role as a source of enrichment. Undue emphasis on the information function may be betting on the wrong horse.

In the library world, consistency rather than change marks the century. The institution has remained and prevailed as a book and print source in an era when communication has gone through successive revolutions. Rather than indicating undue conservatism, this testifies to its essential strength and to the wisdom of its priorities.

Whether this is a promising position from which to enter the next century must still be determined.

## Reprise on Purpose

This history has noted the many additions to the public library's service programs in the twentieth century. Some of these additions and variations have become integral parts of the library and continue to this day, while others were either dropped or pushed into a secondary position. The institution was seemingly searching for an identity or mission and tried many experiments before settling on a core of essential purposes.

The starting point is the typical public library of 1900, a collection of books, mostly subject books which an educated person would like to read, more or less organized for access. It was staffed by caretakers who acquired the materials, kept them in order, and maintained a record of what was taken out.

To this base were added, over the years, many additional resources and services. Here are some examples:

- reference books for factual information
- novels for recreational reading
- children's books for young readers
- subject books for school students
- periodicals for readers of current events
- reference service
- guidance service for children
- guidance service for young adults
- readers' guidance for adults
- branch libraries for convenient access
- rural extension
- classroom collections in schools
- Americanization classes
- promotion of reading by means of reading lists, exhibits, and publicity
- community activities center
- business library service
- subject departmentation
- local history and genealogy
- provision of nonprint materials

Some of these, such as collections in the schools and Americanization classes, existed for only a short time and are no longer in the picture. Others, which were once quite evident, such as adult readers' advisory service, provision of materials for formal students, and serving as a community center, have moved back to second place. Most of the rest were well established by midcentury. The last fifty years did not see as many innovations (except for access to computerized information), but were given more to continuation and improvement of the various existing services and to interlibrary relations to strengthen the delivery of materials sought.

What purposes can be extracted from this panoply of services?

The words that come to mind are education, information, recreation, and guidance. One searches for a single term to characterize the purpose of the public library. Could that term be "enrichment", which in the dictionary definition is "to make richer in quality"? This implies not just information, not just education, not just recreation, but the human outcome of all of these. Here we are somewhere near the central purpose of the library.

Those responsible for the library—staff members, administrators, trustees—accept these aims, even though they cannot readily articulate them. When questioned as to purpose, they are likely to say "well, education, and the other things for which people use reading." Government officials and the general public, are likely to give a similar response. Despite the digital revolution, there remains a faith in the book that is built into the foundation of the library. In the campaign to extend federal aid to libraries in 1963, U.S. Commissioner of Education Frances Keppel, said, "The public library is a basic educational resource. The widespread recognition that education is a life-long process has dramatized the importance of having good library service readily accessible to every citizen."[4]

A Gallup poll in 1993 provides insight into the public view of the agency. A national sample of the general public and a national sample of community leaders were asked to evaluate the value to their communities of ten different roles of the public library.[5] The respondents used categories from "not important" to "very important." More than 80 percent of the general public rated the following roles as "very important."

- Educational support center for students of all ages (88 percent)
- Learning center for adult independent learners (85 percent)
- Discovery and learning center for preschool children (83 percent)

The opinion leaders gave just about the same ratings. Note that all three top roles contain the word educational or learning. Both the general public and the opinion leaders confirm the mission that the public library has claimed for itself—verification for the term "the people's university."

Is "education" what is in the mind of the user who turns to the public library for a travel guide to Spain, a book on recent research on the brain, an account of the Lewis and Clark expedition, a mystery story by P. D. James, a recent issue of a news magazine, or citations for the stock market? Education in any formal sense does not seem to fit such a miscellany of purposes. For this reason the present account uses the overall term of "enrichment." The term encompasses the most formal study on the one side and the reading of a love story on the other.

The respondents in the 1993 poll did not give as high a rating to the informational function as one would expect from its prominence in the current professional literature. This echoes the limited use of the public library for informational purposes which was found way back in the Public Library inquiry at midcentury. The hard reality is that, as we enter the Information Age, the public eye does not see the library as a primary source for hard data. This must be remembered when trying to foresee the role of the public library in the twenty-first century.

Looking back, it is instructive that the public library not only endured but thrived through all the changes of the century. When early in the 1900s everyone was supposed to be out dancing the Charleston, the institution originated some of its most important services. When depression closed in, the public turned to the agency in increasing numbers. During war, information services gained strength. Then after the war, when most people were making their fortunes, large or small, central buildings and branches were constructed. Ideological splits developed in the 1960s in the populace at large, but the public library proceeded to reorganize its governmental base into larger units. Conservatism marked the 1970s but few individuals acquired large libraries; they continued to rely on the public source. The conservative policies of President Reagan entered the picture in the 1980s, but despite some thinned-out budgets, the agency retained much of its financial base.

This resilience was due in the end to general approval of the institution, even by those who never or seldom used it. There is some evidence of an increasing response by the general public. But regular users seldom amount to as much as half of the populace. Who are these regulars? They constitute a very miscellaneous group, from inquiring adults to hard-working students, from business people to housewives, and many in between. Perhaps the only way to characterize the users is to label them "the others"—individuals who go beyond the newspaper and the television to understand the world, individuals seeking to empathize with other human beings beyond the casual contacts of the day, people reaching out mentally and emotionally. Library users are individuals seeking enrichment.

Thus we have an institution that experimented with a variety of services, that early found its essential core, that grew throughout the century on this base, that established itself in the society, and that continues to enjoy widespread popular support. At the same time it is in a sense a marginal institution, at the edge of communication that floods the land in print, in new media, and over the air. It reaches only a minority of the population on a regular basis, and it struggles to gain adequate financial support. The public library at the end of the century is a modest yet established institution that faces a changing world.

## Technology and the Library

To conclude that the public library resisted change in its internal operation would be inaccurate. By 1980 the agency had adopted a variety of technological changes in record handling and in data format and control. These had been coming into the picture before 1980 but spread rapidly during the decade as libraries underwent improvements. The agency was responsive to this degree of change.

The first impact occurred in the keeping of circulation records of materials borrowed from the library. For many years the standard method had depended on a borrower's card, a book card, and a transaction card inserted in a pocket in the book. Each item taken for outside use required hand-stamping of the current date on the several cards. The transaction cards were hand-filed and grouped by date. When the item was returned, the borrower's card was stamped and the transaction card was retrieved from the file. This process was labor-intensive and expensive.

The new method uses automatic scanners attached to automated files. The borrower's card has a stamped code, as does the individual book. Combining the two in the automated file gives a record of the transaction, and a quick scan when the item is returned cancels the transaction records. The issuing of overdue notices is also facilitated from the transaction records that are not canceled. The result is a quick and efficient method which most public libraries have adopted.

Some longtime librarians miss part of the older record that was lost in the change. There is no ready record of the number of items each borrower has, nor is there a ready record in the book of how often it is circulated. Libraries have found that they can live without this information, which can be obtained in separate sampling studies if needed.

Associated with mechanized circulation were new control measures for preventing theft and carelessness in removing items from the building. Sensors at the entrance detect books that have not been neutralized in the circulation process. The sensing equipment sets off an alarm. This technology works to prevent a longstanding problem.

The coming of reduced-size format on microfilm also introduced change, for the microfilm has to be made or purchased and machines to read the film have to be provided. Libraries had been acquiring increasing numbers of periodicals throughout the century and there was demand for back issues. Formerly issues were either filed away by date or bound together by year and placed on the shelves. In either case the full-size holdings consumed more and more space. Microfilm of past issues of journals reduces storage space manyfold. Most libraries now have at least one such reader and larger libraries need a bank of such machines. At times there may be almost as many users at the machines accessing journals and other items as there are regular users working with books at tables.

This improvement does not come without some concern to individual readers. Some members of the public, lacking experience with microfilm, are deterred by this unfamiliar device; staff time is required to show users how to handle the microfilm readers. Others find that it takes extra physical effort to read from the screen. The posture of users sometimes shows this discomfort, but the considerable use of microfilm indicates that the advantages outweigh the disadvantages.

Whether the reduction rate offered by microfilm is what will prevail in the future is a moot point. Technologies exist for a much greater ratio of reduction, and if we are moving toward text in computer memories, the rate of reduction will be increased drastically.

Perhaps the most dramatic of technological change is the computerized catalog. From early times libraries have depended on catalogs in book form and in card form as a means to gain access to the collection. The card catalog listed publications alphabetically by author, by title and by subject. It was time-demanding to maintain and in larger libraries it took on formidable size.

The computer gives the same access and can provide further analysis by subject without increasing the bulk of the record. It can also offer new approaches to showing listings in related subject fields, right down to titles of books on the same shelf, but not many libraries use the full capacity of the computer. One deterrent against more complex analysis is that not enough is known about how different people go about a literature search. This again is a point where the lack of research into use and users limits full exploitation of the tool. The computerized catalog can also be updated everyday, but not all libraries do so in the interest of saving staff time.

Some users are uncomfortable with the computerized catalog. The infrequent visitor is unsure how it works and help is often solicited from the staff; reference librarians find themselves frequently going over the essentials with patrons. Every effort has been made to make a user-friendly catalog and to provide step by step directions, and there is some evidence that more and more users have grown accustomed to it. But the author has more than one friend who says that they avoid the new form; such comments come mostly from older readers.

The most recent technological change is the use of databases accessed by computers. Formerly the librarian (1) identified and acquired the printed manual or reference book, (2) became familiar with its contents when it arrived, and (3) guided the searcher in the use of the resource. With databases, an outside supplier performs these steps. Also, the central computer record can be updated and changed frequently, whereas the reference book, once acquired, sits unrevised on the shelves. Already the local library is an access point (a stop on the Information Highway?) for material built up and maintained away from the building.

In the past a primary reason for maintaining libraries was to have a reservoir of knowledge recorded in print. Few readers had the means or the inclination to maintain their own extensive book libraries. The public library solved the problem for the general public.

Now a parallel service is provided in the computerized services to which the library subscribes. Individuals may gain access for themselves to many of the databases which they need regularly. But what of the many other computerized sources now increasing in numbers? The only free access remains the public library.

Taking the various technical changes as a whole, note that these developments did not alter or effect the priorities of the public library. Rather they aided the agency in what it had been doing; the library went on as before. Both administration and staff have been flexible enough to adopt and administer the modifications but it would be overly sanguine to take this as evidence that the institution has demonstrated that it is ready for the kind of basic change and re-direction that may be needed in the next century.

Thus we have a history of a service that started at the fringe of society, a kind of sideline for a small group of users, and over the years became a built-in institution expected in any organized community. Complexity, education and democracy combined to bring about this change. It is worth noting that the driving force for development came from within localities and not from some national plan or dictated requirement. Step by step the public library added to the kinds of services maintained. Purpose grew from actions taken, mostly in response to local demand, and not from any overall and explicit sense of mission. This is one way for a people's institution to emerge.

## Service to an Aging Population

A principle of public-library service through the years had been to watch for social changes and to respond to adjustments in the community. Toward the end of the century a deep-going change is the increase in the number of older people. Those over sixty-five grew twice as fast as other age groups between 1980 and 1999. By the year 2025 we will have 20 percent of the total population under nineteen years of age, another 20 percent over sixty-five, with the remainder between, and those over fifty increasing in percentage. America is becoming an older society.

Of course there had been senior citizens in earlier decades, and libraries had made some efforts to reach them. For a period delivery service of books to the home had been tried, in part to serve older persons who did not have transportation to the library, but this was uncommon by the 1990s. Some effort was made to work with the senior-citizen centers that were appearing. But serving seniors did not appeal to librarians as much as serving children.

At present, patronage by adults age sixty-five and over may be the lowest of any age group, with perhaps no more than 10 percent of the senior citizens making regular trips to the public library. Yet the potential is there and some libraries—assessing their role in the period ahead—might be wise and foresighted to respond. Here is an opportunity, although it may not have the appeal of getting on the Internet. It is encouraging to see some interest in the prospect: the American Library Association and the National Commission on Library and Information Service hosted a pre-conference session on service to older adults in 1995.

Meeting the challenge will not be easy because several factors mitigate against library use by older people. Some simply have difficulty traveling to the library. Some have limitations in vision, or other handicaps, and many experience a decline in both physical and mental energy. Unfortunately, some senior citizens sit back, fold their hands, take a nap, and lose interest in the world around them.

But this is by no means true for all older people, indeed not for a majority of them. Some are entering the ranks of the retired in their fifties. These and many older are active, curious, and responsive (300,000 every year in elder hostels). They find themselves with the rich gift of time: time to do what stirs them, time to explore lost ground or to venture into new territory. In general the senior citizens are the least educated of adult groups in the society, some having not completed high school back in the early decades, but this picture is changing: only 15 percent of those over 75 have attended college, but the proportion is twice as high for in the age 55 to 64 group.

Older persons potentially have an interest in almost the full range of the library collection. Health, insurance, and investments are subjects that first come mind. Home repair and gardening are not far behind, followed by travel and hobbies. Genealogy and local history catch the interest of others. Some will look back to fill gaps that could not be satisfied when they were working. Now they can read bestsellers that had to be passed by or the classic that earlier seemed too demanding of time. Others will return to an avocational interest, whether the environment or writing or even cooking. Then there is simply reading for diversion, the passing of time when television becomes repetitious. The list is almost endless.

Many libraries have already responded to seniors' demand for large-print books. Besides print, what about books in audio form, on tape, or on CDs, and films and pictorial material? Many seniors, even those living primarily on Social Security checks, have accumulated equipment at home to use these various forms.

But older persons will not automatically come to the library, for they have not been users of the institution. The public library will have to call on its long experience in publicity. Almost all are regular readers of newspapers. They can be reached in senior centers and in retirement homes. It should not be too difficult to build up a mailing list of older persons. They have the time to note the library message. And the retirement communities also provide a convenient contact point. Many seniors feel alone and isolated and seek contacts. Once again the tried-and-true library methods can be used: book talks, book discussion groups, and even book teas. One variation is to pull different age groups together, old and young. What is called for is a mobilization of library methods that have been effective in reaching children and young people, business groups and responsive adults of all ages. There is a discernible and expanding group coming along—senior citizens—a group that now deserves special library attention.

What is required first is an administrative commitment, an agreement to focus and concentrate. More than that there must be advocates, innovators in the staff, even as there were innovators back in the 1920s when basic group services were established. They would be well advised to probe into the habits and problems of their older clientele in order to develop a discipline for their endeavors. Public libraries have tried before to reach distinct population groups—teenagers, business people, less-educated adults—without scouting out the territory and really studying the prospective clientele. As they respond to the older generation, librarians would do well to draw on the growing field of geriatrics. Current library literature is stressing a different emphasis, that on meeting the challenge of digitized information, which we will examine shortly under the heading "The Library in the Sky." Somc professionals will be attracted to the chaos of the Internet and seek to guide searchers lost on the Information Highway. But here in the older generation is a tangible need immediately at hand, a traditional opportunity calling on traditional methods, and some librarians may want to travel this path. Over and above the value to a deserving part of the population, this may help to retain the basic mission of the public library, the role of enrichment.

What should a program for older readers be called? We have had "young peoples service," but "old peoples service" does not seem quite right. The term elder hostel has gained respect. What about "Elderlibra?" Or simply a staff of "senior readers' advisers." One thing can be said for older persons: they will be quick to express gratitude for any service rendered to them.

## The Planning Process

In the 1970s and the 1980s, a significant change of view occurred in the library profession as to how to evaluate public-library service and how to plan for its future. For decades—from 1933 to 1979—the approach had been to project standards which individual libraries were urged to achieve. Deep in the Great Depression, the American Library Association issued fragmentary standards that promulgated the one dollar per capita goal for financial support. The first substantial document of this type was the *Post-War Standards for Public Libraries* (1943) and the last was the *Minimum Standards for Public Library Systems* (1967). There also is a standards statement for children's service.

Sensing that something was lacking in this approach, the Association in 1979 issued the *Public Library Mission Statement*, which sought to focus attention on goals and objectives. There had been notable advance in public-library service in the immediate postwar period—due more to the general prosperity of the country and not to the standards documents in particular—but then progress had slowed in the 1960s before new federal money took effect. The search was on for a new rallying point, a new call to advance.

The assumption behind national standards was that all public libraries—big and small, in manufacturing towns and affluent suburbs, from Miami to Seattle and all centers between—were essentially the same in demand upon them and in what they should provide. The further assumption was that a group of practitioners could be assembled from time to time and could decide upon the kind and level of service that public libraries should provide. In practice, the standards, which were intended as minimum requirements also become maximum levels; once a library came up to the prescribed level it had no further goal to guide it.

Attention shifted to promoting planning within each library in order to establish goals and programs suited to local communities. Standards promoted sameness; the need was for variety and individuality. Thorough planning was designed to break into this comfortable tradition.

The fresh concept of thorough planning in individual libraries would bring service closer to people and introduce a dynamism that critics saw as lacking in library administration. It was believed that this would make for change as needed in service programs rather than for automatic continuation of what had been done in the past. This planning approach would also, it was assumed, make for individuality of programs from library to library, as different agencies and communities would establish their own priorities. The planning process would build in self-examination and self-appraisal.

All administrators engage in planning, planning for the work of the day, and planning for the month or year. This applies to library directors as well as others. But library administrators plan, in a sense, within a groove. They usually assume that what the agency has been doing is what it should continue to do in the future, and that management's job is to carry forward and improve within that framework. The day ends with all the records kept and all the users served, and the year ends with improvement to programs, at which point the administrator considers his or her job done. The administrators stay safely in the groove.

Certain leaders in the field felt that this was not enough. The public library would not achieve its potential, nor would it respond to changed circumstances and new opportunities, if it simply relied on occasional pushing upward of national standards. Officials of the American Library Association joined with these leaders, a grant was obtained through the U.S. Office of Education under the Higher Education Act, Title II B, the Library Research and Demonstration Program, and a decision was made to promote a self-examining planning process within individual libraries.

The result was the *A Planning Process for Public Libraries*.[6] This was prepared on commission by Vernon E. Palmour, then of the King research organization, along with a group of consultants from the library field. The document prescribes seven steps for the planning process:

1. Assessing community library needs.
2. Evaluating current library services and resources.
3. Determining the role of the public library in the community.
4. Setting goals, objectives, and priorities.
5. Developing and evaluating strategies for change.
6. Implementing strategies.
7. Monitoring and evaluating progress towards goals and objectives.

This sequence is to be directed and coordinated by a planning committee within each library composed of staff, trustees, and community members.

Several factors were stressed: the importance of gathering data about the community and the library, the need for establishing goals and priorities, the evaluation of performance, and willingness to consider change. The process is to be thought of as ongoing rather than as a one-shot exercise. In other words, this is planning as it is presented in graduate business programs, planning that is used to vitalize business enterprises.

Over half of the 300-page document is devoted to the gathering of data, community analysis, performance evaluation, and surveys of staff, citizens, and users. One can hardly fault this emphasis, for the present situation must be known, but it sets up a formidable hurdle at the outset and is the reason why many planning programs did not get off the ground.

Use of the document was widely promoted in the 1980s in journal articles, in seminars at annual meetings of the American Library Association, and in visits by state library consultants. A number of libraries carried through the formal planning process, at least once. But several conditions worked against participation. Without outside help, staff did not have the time or skill to gather all the necessary data. Committee members often resisted change, because their own jobs might be involved. Both trustees and community members felt that they were beyond their depth. And the very formality and length of this process were deterrents. This new process—individual planning according to the 1980 document—did not significantly alter or strengthen the American public library.

Once this was recognized, the American Library Association (specifically the Public Library Association, a division of the national organization) pushed for a fresh approach to planning. This time they turned to their own membership and carried out a "Public Library Development Program," resulting in two main documents, *Planning and Role Setting for Public Libraries*[7] and *Output Measures for Public Libraries*.[8] The first of these takes off from the Palmour manual of 1980 and the second from work done by De Prospo[9] and Zweizig in the 1970s.

The new planning document was designed as a self-help manual. The process was outlined step by step. Research required to obtain background data was simplified. The result is a user-friendly guide, yet one that retains the basic aim of local self-examination and decision making.

The new concept in the document is that of role setting. With data in hand about both the community and the library, the planners are to select among possible roles for the agency, accepting some and rejecting others, and then setting priorities among those that are accepted. Eight roles are suggested:

1. community activities center;
2. community information center;
3. formal education support center;
4. independent learning center;
5. popular materials library;
6. preschoolers' door to learning;

7. reference library;
8. research center.

Role setting is the nub of the matter. Here is where the hard decisions should be made. This is not supposed to be simply a record of what the library is doing now, but rather a commitment to what it should be doing, what it will seek to be in the period ahead. It is an attempt to answer the question: what should be our business in the Information Age? Actually there is an escape hatch here; a library has simply to accept all or most of the roles and it will be back where it is now.

But if planning and role setting is done faithfully and realistically, the path ahead should become clear. The decisions can then be put into a mission statement and then into goals and objectives to guide budget making, staffing, space disposition, and service efforts. Such planning could turn an agency around and refocus its program.

The output measures come into the process at a later stage. Then an evaluation can be done to see what has been accomplished. An evaluation can also be used independently of planning and role setting, in judging an on-going service program, but their special value is when new directions are taken and the question is what has been achieved by so doing.

These measures are also a break with the past standards where the emphasis was on input—what should go into an effective library program. Instead of financial support, number of staff, and size of collection, the spotlight is now on what these inputs produce. The output measures focus on browsers' fill rate, reference completion rate, and request fill rate, what users go out with when they leave the library—the bottom line, the units produced, the sales record.

The new planning and the output measures have been used to some extent in public libraries, but they certainly have not led to a revolution or much discernible change in the agency. Perhaps the new approach still needs testing. But the role-setting document was issued over a decade ago (1987), and recent reports of its use are infrequent. Is this another ill-fated effort to push the institution to planning for the period ahead?

There are alternative strategies for trying to break out of the mold and achieving change for future demands. Rather than going through the whole planning process, library administrators could individually take the plunge and propose basic change, and then seek to carry along trustees, staff, and community. This would be an act of old-fashioned leadership (like John Shaw Billings in the early 1900s, John Cotton Dana in the 1920s, Joseph Wheeler in the 1930s, and Carleton Joeckel in the 1940s), which provides someone out in front to rally those behind.

For example, priority attention to and provision for supplying of information could be proposed, even though other goals would have to be cut back, on the grounds that this is needed to keep the institution vital in the Information Age. Or another possible emphasis would be to stress the adult-education role, in this case on the grounds that this is a still-needed function which both the library and the society have put on the sidelines. Everything would then depend on the leadership of the library administrator to achieve the new emphasis. The question here is whether the staff would follow the fresh lead.

Another alternative strategy is to call in an outside consultant who would go through the planning process and come out with recommendations. This approach has been used by some city libraries over the years, in some cases with enough impact to provide direction and renewed dedication. In this case, however, everything depends on the insight and persuasiveness of one outsider.

The foundation of communication and information is changing. Every library should be devoting part of its energy to planning. The agency that does not is asking for trouble. It should reexamine its role and it may conclude that some essential adjustments are in order.

As the public library moves toward a new century, it is easy on the one hand to identify the influences that will keep it very much as it is, and not easy on the other hand to detect the stimulants that will move the institution to its next stage of development. In the next section of this history an effort will be made to propose what the public library can and should do for the years ahead.

## The Library in the Sky

Early and late, the demise of the library has been predicted.

"Libraries as we know them are on the way out. We are destined to have libraries without halls or walls, libraries that lack stacks."[10]

Earlier the same prediction was made in these terms: "our present libraries will be obsolete by 2,000 A.D."[11] More recently the formulation was: "libraries would wither away, their historic duty done."[12]

The favored date for the end of the library was the year 2000. Yet here we are at the end of the century and the institution is very much with us, and in fact new buildings with extended book shelves are being built. Were the prognosticators wrong, or the librarians oblivious of what is happening around them? The following analysis will present one view, and it is presented with recognition that the crystal ball is murky and the future of the computer unpredictable.

It may help to divide the discussion into the three purposes that have consistently appeared for the public library—information, education, and recreation. Different conclusions may be reached by taking up each of these functions in turn.

The advantage of on-line information is self-evident. The reference books on the library's shelves are sometimes partially out of date by the time they are printed and acquired, whereas the digitized database can be updated regularly. The amount and scope of library information is circumscribed by what stands on the shelves, whereas the information in databases and the Internet is almost without limits. Electronic communication makes it unnecessary for the searcher and the source to be in the same location or working at the same time. Data drawn from faraway networks can be delivered when the user is not even at home and accumulated for later examination. The visit to the library—when it is open—is avoided.

Libraries subscribe to some of the data sources and will no doubt seek to gain access to others. This has already changed the agency and has increased the resources available to the librarian. So far the library seems strengthened rather than diminished as a result.

But a few pointed questions must be raised. If computer terminals are available in the office and at home, wouldn't the information seeker dial direct to the database without going through the library? For these equipped searchers, that would seem to be the logical approach, and it would not require any use of the library.

Will those who don't have the necessary hardware—the "have-nots"—turn to the library? At this juncture we must remind ourselves that the Public Library inquiry at midcentury and other studies since then have shown that the general public, with or without computers, does not turn naturally to the public library for factual information.[13] It is possible that the "haves" will seek out the agency when they want access to databases to which they do not subscribe, even as book owners now turn to the library when they want to go beyond what is on their own shelves. As to the "have-nots," one should note the Libraries Online! project launched jointly by the American Library Association and the Microsoft Corporation in 1996 to bring information service to the "others."[14] Through this project, the corporation contributes financial and software assistance to over two hundred library systems to provide economically disadvantaged communities access to the Internet. Other cities and states are taking similar steps, so now a majority of public libraries provide access to the Internet.

These are efforts to connect digital information to what are termed "underserved populations." No doubt the technical connection can be made, but what will supply the general populations to seek out data now that it is in computerized form when they did not do so when it was in book form?

There is another possibility for the library at the time when all seekers have direct access to databases. These sources increase in number constantly, as does the complexity of the Internet. Users may well need and seek guidance on navigating through the "library in the sky." The librarian may become both the interpreter and the adviser. Staff members have served in this capacity in guiding readers in using the many books on the shelves and might serve similarly in the realm of remote sources.

Information seekers might consult with librarians about the Internet much like individuals consult with lawyers about the intricacies of the law. More dramatic terms have been applied to the librarian of the future. A conference in 1996 came up with the terms "Cybrarian" and "Gate Keeper,"[15] and then there are "knowledge navigator" and "database manager." But there is merit in the longstanding term "librarian," the professional who knows the resources of a library.

Librarians are already becoming familiar with the new digital sources. However, this history has more than once referred to the limited amount of research that has been done on readers and reading, thus limiting the effectiveness of librarians as readers' advisers. Now there is a similar limitation in understanding how information seekers proceed and how successful they are in reaching their goals. Until librarians become more familiar with how people seek and use information, they will not be turned to by substantial portions of the population for guidance on how to reach out to the new resources. It is not too much to hope that graduate library schools (many of which have added "information" to their titles) will dig in, become creative, and fill this void in the professional background; if this were to occur, universities might look with more favor on their library schools.

Actually it is doubtful whether we are entering a new age that requires information; that need has been there all the time. What we are seeing is new means of recording and communicating factual data. This is a significant step forward, and these new media will flourish in these next years, but this does not automatically transform the library into a primary information source. What it does is provide sources in addition to the library, over and above what stands in the collection.

So, on information provision through libraries, we are left with an uncertain future. A realistic appraisal of the prospect raises more questions than answers.

If the public in general learns to depend on the library as a primary source of information, and if librarians learn more about how people use information, the public library will move into the forefront in fact provision. Note that this statement has two "if" conditions, and note that neither is significantly coming to pass. Neither the receiver nor the supplier have as yet come closer together. Until they do, many inquirers will remain in ignorance and many librarians will wait passively.

In summary, it is unlikely that libraries will become a primary source of digitized information since computer owners have direct access to resources. There may be some printed reference books that libraries will still supply, mostly those providing historical facts, but most contemporary data sources will be outside of the library. There may be a role for the librarian to serve as the recognized guide to this remote library, but only if senior reference librarians come to fully understand this new information-seeking process. On the information front, the prospect is uncertain and problematical. Unless basic adjustments are made, the public library will not be a primary source of information in the twenty-first century, any more than it has been so in the past one hundred years.

This conclusion may be troubling to librarians, who had hoped to be in the forefront of the Information Age, but it is one realistic reading of the crystal ball.

Turning to the variety of services that have been termed "educational," the prospect is quite different and more favorable. Here we are back where the public library started and back with the role that has carried it through the twentieth century. Will it also sustain the agency in the next period?

Education is a broad term with varied meanings. At one extreme it is a formal class under a teacher but at the other extreme it is an individual sitting quietly at home reading about trouble in the Middle East. The latter also is education, with a learner, a goal, and the means to bring the two together in the form of a book. The purpose here is not facts, information in the narrow sense, but understanding, knowing, analyzing, even feeling. The scenario could be duplicated many fold, with individuals seeking to understand any of the myriad topics which the human mind can dream up.

The digital champion might point out that the library—at least as we have known it—is still not necessary. Going through the computer, the reader could request the necessary book or books from the library in the sky. After all, it will not be too long before all books in the Library of Congress will be in digital form. The pages of the volume would come back to the computer screen, would be put into print on pages in the adjacent printer, and then fastened together in the shape of a book. There would be no library, no collection, no book, at least in the traditional form.

But here the old-fashioned reader could raise a hard question. If we are going to buy all the necessary equipment, build a library in the sky, use the electronic channels, and eventually end up with words on a page, why not simply have the book in the first place?

Thus we come back to the library, doing what it has been doing for a century or more. If the database is the source of information, the library will remain the source of knowledge.

Trends in the society will increase demand for sources of

knowledge. The average educational level of the population is steadily increasing. More and more jobs require subject knowledge, whether of technical subjects, group relations, psychological factors, or international relations. With greater life expectancy, older people are spending one-third of their lives in "retirement," often with alert minds and curiosity about the world. Neither a larger Internet nor more television channels will meet their needs.

The library's educational function remains a challenge, as it has in the past. It will call upon insight in provision of printed sources, in organizing materials for use, and in advising users—which is what this history has been about. Genuine professional prospects abound, off the Information Highway.

The recreation function of the library has been something of a neglected child in the family. All public libraries have some publications for diversion and recent issues many even be placed prominently in display cases. But professional literature does not highlight this function; it is not featured in ALA's Goals 2000, nor is it stressed when seeking financial support. Librarians are a little apologetic about this function. The plain child of recreation is not pushed forward in family portraits.

Yet a case can be made that the fiction section serves a deep human need. It is interesting and surprising, in reading what has become almost the handbook of the Digital Age, to come on these sentences:

> Interactive multimedia leaves very little to the imagination. . . . By contrast, the written word sparks images and evokes metaphors that get much of their meaning from the reader's imagination and experiences. When you read a novel, much of the color, sound, and motion come from you.[16]

Imagination, fancy, thinking—these give the meaning to recreation.

Would one give this quality to the novels of Judith Krantz and her ilk? For some people, yes. So if this is not your brand of diversion, try the short stories of John Cheever or the poetry of Stanley Kunitz or the novels of Toni Morrison. Or read *To Kill a Mockingbird* again and feel the warmth in your heart.

Note the reference in the quotation from Negroponte to the role of metaphor.

Go back to Emily Dickinson:

> To make a prairie it takes a clover and one bee,
> One clover, and a bee,
> And revery,
> The revery alone will do,
> If bees are few.

Quiet contemplation of these lines may or may not be "recreation," but it is different from what comes out of the database.

Providing books and periodicals for recreation in all its variety is not only a worthy function, but in a busy and tense age may be a necessity. In this domain individuals may exercise their human qualities to the fullest. The neglected child should be taken from the kitchen and put up front in the living room. Public libraries might even have senior staff in the role of recreation readers' advisers.

Throughout this history the concept of enrichment was featured as an underlying purpose of the library. This does not exclude provision of information, for a person is enriched with accurate factual data. The public library should have a place on the Information Highway but it should also come off the big road and visit the green countryside. It has had and will continue to have a significant niche in promoting understanding. And it has had and could enlarge its role in providing recreation, even for those who come back from cyberspace.

It is indicative that when Bill Gates, who made a fortune in designing computer software, wanted to convey his view of what has transpired to now and what will occur next, when he wanted to communicate to the wider audience, chose the book form to do so. Indeed, after all the discussion of bits and bytes, he makes a confession: "the paper-based book, magazine or newspaper has a lot of advantages over its digital counterpart."[17] The advantages he cites are that the book is small, lightweight, high resolution and inexpensive. One might add that it is also more flexible, more analytical, and more inspirational.

All this sounds like a vindication of the traditional public-library program, a reaffirmation of what the agency has been doing all along. To an extent this is true, for the conclusion here points towards an institution serving the human interest in knowledge, in diversion, and in factual data, with emphasis on the first of these. But another way of putting this is that the public library must hold to the essentials that have carried it through a century of growth and gained it public approval. The agency has been serving fundamental human needs, and these needs will not change when we sit down at a computer or when the year 1999 comes to an end.

The public library has served three broad areas of public interest: the world of ideas, the world of creative expression, and the world of information. Of the three, the American Library Association Goal 2000 plan has selected and attached itself to the information function. This of course is worthy in itself, but it may not be the wisest choice for the twenty-first century. The information sphere is where the greatest competition is occurring; the computer and the Internet are formidable adversaries. At the same time the world of ideas and creative expression will go on, not capturing the headlines as often nor gaining as much governmental attention. The public library has been a mainstay in serving these other worlds. Is this something that we do not need in the twenty-first century?

In a sense the public library has been an institution ahead of its time. Early in the century it established a service program based on the assumption of a populace thirsting for knowledge and prepared to devote time and attention to gaining insight and wisdom. But early on this was true of only a minor part of the adult population. These exceptional individuals sought out the agency but did not constitute a large user group. The library therefore added recreational reading, children's service, fact provision, and group activities in an effort to broaden its social base. It was able to present these various efforts under the rubric of "education."

But now we have a more educated population. Is this also a more alert and motivated population that has caught up with the knowledge agency that has been in its midst all these years? It is possible to make this case, and to the extent that it can be made the best years for the public library are ahead. This is not a future dependent on computers and the Internet. It is based on a vision of a prosperous people still seeking to understand themselves and the world around them. This assumption is based on more evidence than was available a century ago. We have in the public library an established institution devoted not primarily to information but to understanding and appreciation. For an agency engaged in the business of enrichment, the best years may be ahead.

The public library will provide enrichment well into the twenty-first century. And it will do so primarily with the medium of the printed page. Without it we will all be the poorer. The history of the public library highlights an essential role that will be needed more, not less, in our future.

## Notes

1. Peter Brimlow, *The Alien Nation* (New York: Random House, 1995).

2. Paul Kennedy, *The Rise and Fall of the Great Powers* (New York: Random House, 1987).

3. *New York Times*, 25 March, 1996, A1.

4. Edward G. Holley, *The Library Services and Construction Act* (Greenwich, Conn.: JAI Press, 1983), 61.

5. *The Bowker Annual Library and Book Trade Almanac, 1994* (New Providence, N.J.: R. R. Bowker, 1994), 430–32.

6. Vernon E. Palmour, *A Planning Process for Public Libraries* (Chicago: American Library Association, 1980).

7. Charles R. McClure, *Planning and Role Setting in Public Libraries* (Chicago: American Library Association, 1987).

8. Douglas Zweizig, *Output Measures for Public Libraries: A Manual of Standardized Procedures* (Chicago: American Library Association, 1982).

9. Ernest DeProspo, *Performance Measures for Public Libraries* (Chicago: American Library Association, 1973).

10. Talat S. Halman, "From Babylon to Cyberspace," in *American Libraries*, vol. 26 (1995), 895.

11. John G. Kemeny, "A Library for 2,000 A.D.," in Martin Greenberger, ed. *Computers and the World of the Future*. (Boston: MIT Press, 1962), 159.

12. H. Folk, "The Impact of Computers on Book and Journal Publication," in J. L. Divilbliss, ed. *The Economics of Library Automation* (Urbana, Ill.: University of Illinois Press, 1977), 79.

13. See, for example, Douglas Zweizig, "Public Library Use, Users, Uses," in Melven Voight, ed. *Advances in Librarianship* (New York: Academic Press, 1977), 236.

14. "ALA, Microsoft Launch Libraries on Line." *American Libraries* vol. 27, (1996), 7.

15. *New York Times*, 29 April, 1996, A21.

16. Nicholas Negroponte, *Being Digital* (New York: Knopf, 1995), 8.

17. Bill Gates, *The Road Ahead* (New York: Viking, 1995), 113.

# Bibliography

This is a selective list. Literally thousands of other items in the extensive literature of librarianship bear upon the story, but these are the substantial landmark publications that add a new development or distinctive viewpoint to the history of the institution.


*American Library Association. Minimum Standards for Public Library Systems*. Chicago: American Library Association, 1967.

American Library Association. *Post-War Standards for Public Libraries*. Chicago: American Library Association, 1943.

American Library Association. *Public Library Mission Statement*. Chicago: American Library Association, 1979.

Ballard, Thomas H. *The Failure of Resource Sharing in Public Libraries and Alternative Strategies of Service*. Chicago: American Library Association, 1986.

Berelson, Bernard. *The Library's Public*. New York: Columbia University Press, 1949.

Bobinski, George E. *Carnegie Libraries: Their History and Impact on American Library Development*. Chicago: American Library Association, 1969.

Boorstin, Daniel J. *The Democratic Experience*. New York: Random House, 1973.

Bostwick, Arthur E. *The American Public Library*. New York: Appleton, 1929.

Braverman, Miriam. *Youth, Society, and the Public Library*. Chicago: American Library Association, 1979.

Bryan, Alice I. *The Public Librarian*. New York: Columbia University Press, 1949.

Chelton, Mary K. *Excellence in Library Services to Young Adults*. Chicago: American Library Association, 1994.

Chisholm, Margaret (ed.). *Reader in Media, Technology and Libraries*. Englewood, Colo.: Microcard Editions Books, 1975.

Danton, Emily. *Pioneering Leaders in Libraries*. Chicago: American Library Association, 1953.

De Prospo, Ernest. *Performance Measure for Public Libraries*. Chicago: American Library Association, 1973.

Ditzion, Sidney. *Arsenals of a Democratic Culture: A Social History of the American Public Library Movement in New England and Middle States from 1850–1900*. Chicago: American Library Association, 1947.

Garceau, Oliver. *The Public Library in the Political Process*. New York: Columbia University Press, 1949.

Garrison, Dee. *Apostles of Culture; The Public Librarian and the American Society, 1876–1920*. New York: Free Press, 1970.

Gates, Bill. *The Road Ahead*. New York: Viking, 1995.

Gertzog, Alice, and Edwin Beckerman *Administration of the Public Library*. Metuchen, N.J.: Scarecrow Press, 1994.

Gleason, Eliza A. *The Southern Negro and the Public Library*. Chicago: University of Chicago Press, 1941.

Harris, Michael H. *History of Libraries in the Western World*. Metuchen, N.J.: Scarecrow Press, 1995.

Harris, Michael H. (ed.). *Reader in American Library History*. 4th ed. Washington, D.C.: Microcard Editions, 1971.

Holley, Edward G. *The Library Services and Construction Act*. Greenwich, Conn.: JAI Press, 1983.

Holt, Raymond A. *Planning Library Buildings and Facilities; From Concept to Completion*. Metuchen, N.J.: Scarecrow Press, 1989.

Jackson, Sidney L. *A Century of Service*. Chicago: American Library Association, 1976.

Joeckel, Carleton B., and Amy Winslow. *A National Plan for Public Library Service*. Chicago: American Library Association, 1948.

Josey, E. J. *Politics and the Support of Libraries*. New York: Neal-Schuman, 1990.

Ladenson, Alex. *Library Law and Legislation in the United States*. Metuchen, N.J.: Scarecrow Press, 1982.

Lancaster, F. W. *The Measurement and Evaluation of Library Services*. Washington, D.C.: Information Resources Press, 1977.

Lee, Robert E. *Continuing Education for Adults Through the American Public Library, 1833–1964*. Chicago: American Library Association, 1966.

Leigh, Robert D. *The Public Library in the United States*. New York: Columbia University Press, 1950.

McClure, Charles R. *Planning and Role Setting in Public Libraries*. Chicago: American Library Association, 1987.

Moneypenny, Philip. *The Library Functions of the States*. Chicago: American Library Association, 1966.

Monroe, Margaret. *Library Adult Education: The Biography of an Idea*. Metuchen, N.J.: Scarecrow Press, 1963.

Negroponte, Nicholas. *Being Digital*. New York: Knopf, 1995.

Nelson Associates. *Public Library Systems in the United States*. Chicago: American Library Association, 1969.

Palmour, Vernon E. *A Planning Process for Public Libraries*. Chicago: American Library Association, 1980.

Rollock, Barbara B. *Library Services for Children*. Hamden, Conn.: Library Professional Publications, 1988.

Schenk, Gretchen K. *County and Regional Library Development*. Chicago: American Library Association, 1954.

Shera, Jesse. *Foundations of the Public Library*. Chicago: University of Chicago, 1949.

VanSlyck, Abigail A. *Free to All: Carnegie Libraries and American Culture, 1890–1920*. Chicago: University of Chicago Press, 1996.

Voight, Melvin (ed.). *Advances in Librarianship*. New York: Academic Press, 1977.

Wall, Joseph E. *Andrew Carnegie*. New York: Oxford University Press, 1970.

Wheeler, Joseph L., and Alfred M. Githens. *The American Public Library Building*. New York: Scribner, 1941.

Wiegand, Wayne A. *An Active Instrument of Propaganda: The American Public Library During World War I*. New York: Greenwood Press, 1989.

Williams, Patrick. *The American Public Library and the Problem of Purpose*. New York: Greenwood Press, 1988.

Williamson, Charles. *Training for Library Service*. Boston: Merrymount Press, 1923.

Zweizig, Douglas. *Output Measures for Public Libraries: A Manual of Standardized Procedures*. Chicago: American Library Association, 1982.

# Index

# About the Author

**Lowell A. Martin** (B.S., Illinois Institute of Technology; Ph.D., University of Chicago) has worked in libraries, library schools, and in publishing. He was branch librarian and assistant to the chief librarian, Chicago Public Library; professor and associate dean, School of Library Service, Columbia University; and organizer and dean of the library school at Rutgers University. Dr. Martin was vice president of Grolier, Inc., a publisher of reference books. In recent years he has conducted administrative surveys of several city libraries in Chicago, Los Angeles, San Francisco, Atlanta, Dallas, Philadelphia, Baltimore, and Portland. He is the author of *Library Response to Urban Change* (American Library Association, 1969).